TECHNO-CRAZED

CRAZED

THE

BUSINESSPERSON'S

GUIDE TO

CONTROLLING

TECHNOLOGY—

BEFORE IT

CONTROLS YOU

MICHAEL FINLEY

PETERSON'S/PACESETTER BOOKS
PRINCETON, NEW JERSEY

Many ideas in this book were explored in different form in Michael Finley's column "On the Edge" in the *St. Paul Pioneer Press* and other Knight-Ridder Newspapers.

Other material appeared in *Computer User, Maximize, Portable Computing, Corporate Computing, Business Computing,* and other publications.

Techno-Crazed is published by Peterson's/Pacesetter Books.

Pacesetter Books, Peterson's/Pacesetter Books, and the Pacesetter horse design are trademarks of Peterson's Guides, Inc.

Library of Congress Cataloging-in-Publication Data

Finley, Michael, 1950—
    Techno-crazed : the businessperson's guide to controlling technology—before it controls you / Michael Finley.
        p.   cm.
    ISBN 1-56079-570-0
    1. Information technology—Management.   2. Information superhighway.   I. Title.
HD30.2.F56   1995
658.4'038—dc20   95-18847
                                                                                CIP

Creative direction by Linda Huber
Cover design by Irving Freeman Design Co.
Interior design by Cynthia Boone

Printed in the United States of America

10 9 8 7 6 5 4 3 2 1

Visit Peterson's Education Center on the Internet (World Wide Web) at
http://www.petersons.com

I dedicate this book to two old-timer authors who reshaped my thinking long ago . . .

To Alvin Toffler, whose book *Future Shock*, published when I was in college in 1972, told me that technology no longer belonged solely to technocrats—we were all entitled to have our say.

And to Peter McWilliams, whose whimsical and very readable *The Personal Computer Book* filled me back in 1981 with a hunger to have one of them things, and told me that even poets could play this game.

CONTENTS

ACKNOWLEDGMENTS

This book wasn't my idea. I was minding my own business, writing a column for the *St. Paul Pioneer Press*, when Andrea Pedolsky, my editor at Peterson's/Pacesetter Books, proposed the concept to me: a book called *Techno-Crazed* that would look at computing from a human perspective. I had been writing about technology from that perspective for several years, so the book seemed like a good fit.

Andrea is very smart and very confident, and she soon imparted a kernel of her confidence in me, a notorious pessimist. As to smartness, she left me to fend for myself. I'm honored by her trust and grateful for her reassurance and brow-fanning at key intervals.

Others at Peterson's/Pacesetter Books also helped in big ways: Lenore Greenberg, Martha Kemplin, Bernadette Boylan, and Gary Rozmierski. Thanks to my friend and professional indexer Diana Witt for straightening out my back matter. Thanks, everyone.

Hats off as well to Mike Peluso, business editor with the *St. Paul Pioneer Press*, and managing editor Ken Doctor, who commissioned the column. Writing a weekly column in your hometown is great fun. If you are lucky enough to be in St. Paul, Minnesota, by all means read the *Pioneer Press*. It's an *excellent* newspaper.

Here's to Kevin Reichard, who invited me to write about technology for the *Computer User* national tabloid chain eight years ago. It was a brave, crazy, dubious idea: I knew nothing about computers except that they were interesting to me. From such a slender thread hangs all that has come to pass.

Thanks to my other sage editors: Hilory Wagner, Michael Comendul, and George Bond at *Maximize/IDG*, Steve Deyo with *Computer User*, Eileen Feretic at IBM's *Beyond Computing*, and Rochelle Garner and Pat Houston of Ziff-Davis's now-defunct *Corporate Computing*.

Thanks to The Masters Forum, a Twin Cities executive education group I write for, for giving me the time and space to complete this project.

Thanks to my two great friends and fellow ink-stained wretches, Jerry de Jaager and Jim Thornton, who read the book for me at the eleventh minute and helped me make it better. Jerry, my co-editor at The Masters Forum, was an icon (in the old sense) of sympathy and supportiveness. Jim and I have been shackled together for years like Laurel and Hardy—he is the funny, innocent one, and I am the fat, exasperated one—and we would be friends even if our young sons were not. These guys are like the spider in *Charlotte's Web*—loyal friends who can also write—and I am grateful to them.

Thanks to Paul Finley, my dad, who read excerpts of this book and declared it bathroom ready. "The sections are the perfect length," he said.

Thanks also to another friend, sometime collaborator and business psychologist Harvey Robbins, who with me and Andrea created *Why Teams Don't Work* (Peterson's/Pacesetter Books, 1995), and who has patiently waited on the sidelines till I finished my solo book and returned to our team.

Thanks to all the people on my favorite hometown BBSes that gave me ideas and support, the people of the Twin Cities Citadel bulletin boards. Citadel isn't a famous BBS software, but I love it, because it's easy and fast and allows the kind of rapid-fire exchange of a real conversation. Thanks to Hue White Jr. for developing and maintaining it, and to sysops Dave Marquette (Topper), Bob Marz (Remi Fasolati), Mary Herman (mary mary) and Jim Moore (Jimbo) for their hospitality over the last ten years. And to all the BBSers that I may seldom or never meet but who have been my friends and companions in an otherwise lonely profession.

Thanks to the people of the Usenet newsgroups, especially the curmudgeonly crowd at alt.folklore.computers. Their posts about end-user stupidity were simultaneously enlightening, dismaying, and hilarious. Thanks to Rand Lindsly and the many netriders who contributed quotes from databases on the World Wide Web.

I apologize also if I have repeated a misattribution or credited the wrong speaker, although I must point out that such errors bolster the point I make somewhere in this book that proper credit in an era of free-flowing data can be awfully hard to obtain.

Finally, I would be remiss and in really big trouble if I overlooked my superfine wife and best friend Rachel and our blue-ribbon offspring, Daniele and Jonathan. They know better than anyone the true depths of my Techno Craziness, have suffered through it with me and, from all appearances, have forgiven me. Unless they have really long memories and have something truly grisly planned for me, which I hope they don't.

How to Read This Book

Every author would love a review that says, "I couldn't put it down!" My hope, however, is that readers do not zip through *Techno-Crazed* in one sitting. It is a book of essays, a grab bag of ideas with shifting moods and emphases. By turns silly and solemn, it is a series of sprints—not a marathon trudge. Readers are encouraged to read nonlinearly. Open it up and start anywhere, like the *Guinness Book of Records*. If I could recommend one room of the house in which to read it, I'd have to go with the bath.

INTRODUCTION
It and Us
Living with Technology

I recently wrote a column calling for a new approach to teaching people how to run software. The gist of this argument is that the makers of technology are doing their best on their side of the equation to make products easy to use, and users (most of them, anyway) are doing their best on their side of the equation to learn from the materials provided to them.

What each side needs to do, the column suggested, is try harder to understand and appreciate the position of the other side. Customers need to work to overcome their resistance to reading documentation and to learn how to think more like a computer; computer and software makers need to create new-generation, custom documentation that addresses the needs of individual users.

In my mind the column was a paragon of balance, favoring neither side. But when I posted it to a Usenet newsgroup frequented by technology people, some of the denizens of that place erupted, flaming me with pure techie venom. They felt I was taking the side of "moronic" customers over decent, hard-working techies. Here's one reply, which is insulting in the way that only indignant Internet old-timers can be:

> Oh, come on Mike.
>
> You are just the most recent example of a clueless journalist, having discovered the Internet or being told to discover the Internet, who logs in and posts a truly stupid flamebait. You get deservedly flamed, so you go out and write EXACTLY the story you intended to write in the first place.
>
> Having totally failed in grasping a clue, you pat yourself on the back and tell yourself and your readers that all those folks who have spent years and years learning computers are real mean SOBs simply because YOU and your readers are too damned lazy and stupid to crack a book.
>
> In this, you are not at all different from the pitiful folks who refuse to learn to drive, operate a TV, use a telephone, etc. etc.

Technology has passed you by and made your education obsolete. The typical 12-year-old is more technology savvy than you are and is more fit to survive in a technological society. Like any other endangered species, this leaves you frightened, bewildered, and very angry.

Since you don't have the intellectual honesty to direct your anger at the REAL target—yourself and your lack of education—you make the usual pathetic attempt to target the bearers of the ugly message in the usual human tradition.

Sorry, but I don't feel sorry for you. If your current employer expects computer literacy, before you make the obvious career move, you need to be aware that McDonald's is a very, very high-tech job workplace.

You had the opportunity to do your readers a service by pointing out that the state of today's technology is such that a bit of education IS REQUIRED—further, that if they wish to prosper in that society, sooner or later they can expect to run into this problem.

> "Never let a computer know you're in a hurry."
>
> *Anonymous*

If you had any real research credentials and reasoning ability, you would be aware that no matter how easy ANY technology is to use, there will always be newer technology constantly emerging. Those who stay abreast survive and prosper. Those who don't stay naked and huddle in caves and freeze to death because they refuse to learn how to make spearheads and arrowheads. Those societies who simply pull a "Mike Finley" and kill the arrowhead-maker sooner or later, deservedly, become extinct.

At least you can rest easy knowing that the phrase "Mike Finley" is very likely to gain the same level of recognition on the Internet as that of Ned Ludd and his ilk.

In a few years, rather than posting about "lusers," we will all be posting about "Mike-Finley-users" and their stupidity.

You, hopefully, will be sorting through trashcans or sitting on a branch with the spotted owl—which is more than you deserve.

Techies as a class have the reputation of sitting on their feelings, but not this fellow. And he's right. Ordinary people are expecting that the tools painstakingly developed over centuries by people of the caliber of Leibniz, Babbage, and von Neumann—who never in their wildest dreams imagined anything like the personal computers we use today—should be as easy to use as a vacuum cleaner. It makes perfect sense that such a collision of purposes—theirs and ours—would result in grotesque pain for both sides.

Which leaves the vast middle of us right there, in the middle, and feeling stress because of the contradiction between the superficial simplicity of Windows 95 or the Mac interface or What-You-See-Is-What-You-Get word processing or Microsoft "Bob" and the dizzying 12-diskette depth of detail just below the surface.

Even when computer science tries to appear simple for our benefit, it masks a frightful complexity. What is simplicity, anyway? Could any two of us ever agree on what that simplicity would be like? The best we could do is supply vague hints, unsystematic wish lists that could vary widely from user to user. To a teacher of Boolean algebra, it might be a keyboard with two keys, 0 and 1. All digital technology does, after all, is sort 0s from 1s. But to us that would be a very unyielding kind of simplicity, like the monolith that the ape race at the dawn of time in *2001: A Space Odyssey* could only screech at and beat on. The design of simplicity is left to the masters of complexity, and rightly so.

This is the tension that makes us crazy. When systems go down, we hope our slender thread of knowledge will help us. It seldom does. Technology leads even the cleverest of our ape race around on a tether. We may flatter ourselves that we get it, because we know how to select bullets of different shapes or get the decimal points to line up in the tables we create. Then, when technology throws us for a loop, we feel betrayed—the thread of knowledge we were so proud of unravels in our hands.

This moment could go either way. My techie letter-writer wishes we would either commit to learning technology at the high level he has,

> If the automobile had followed the same development cycle as the computer, a Rolls-Royce would today cost $100, get a million miles per gallon, and explode once a year, killing everyone inside."
>
> *Robert X. Cringely*[1]

or else (this is my opinion) we should just go away and let him and his techie buddies play with their toys.[2]

Technology will always be too hard for some people. A few of us will never be willing to do the work necessary to become competent at our consoles. The guaranteed-100-percent-no-brainer computer of the future may go on sale at Wal-Mart some day, but everyone reading this will be dead by then.

Despite an ocean of misgivings and caterwauling, we are moving toward effortless, zero-training computing. Systems are ten times easier to use today than they were ten years ago, in some ways. That is good news. The bad news is, we ain't there yet. And we may never be truly happy with our tools. I doubt there will ever be a state of zero disparity between us and our machines, until we hardwire them into our cerebral cortices, an option I heartily recommend in Chapter 10.

> "A PC is like an Old Testament God. Lots of rules, and absolutely no mercy."
>
> *Joseph Campbell*[3]

So the logical course of action is to accept that there will always be some degree of difficulty. It will always make us a little crazy. Short of taking a 50-year nap and awakening in the idiot-proof future, we have no real alternative except to learn, each of us in our own way, to live with whatever conditions currently prevail.

MY STEPDAD, DICK

I got interested in computers fifteen years ago. The Apple II was a sensation, Radio Shack was selling machines in shopping malls, the IBM PC was just around the corner, and writer friends were abuzz about the new "word processors" that were coming out. I was writing a book at the time, and each revision had to be laboriously retyped on a Hermes steel typewriter. I knew it didn't have to be this way—a year earlier, I'd worked on a newspaper that had word processing terminals and I was in awe of their ability to save and edit files and to move around blocks of text.

That meant no more retyping, a godsend to all writers like me who on a good day type maybe ten words per minute. It spelled an end to the drudgery of writing. I promised myself I would use the proceeds from that first book to buy an Apple II or a TRS-80.

Fifteen years and about as many books later, I have exchanged the Hermes 3000 for a 486 PC clone—my sixth computer, counting portables. Though I am no techie and quickly get lost when talk takes a turn for the technical, I have a generally good feeling about machines and programs. But I know very well that many people don't feel that way.

My stepdad, Dick, was a great guy who owned a small trucking and excavating company near Cleveland. Dick ran his business on an informal, family, first-name basis. He often paid in cash and was paid in cash. His whole enterprise ran on a handshake basis. And he loathed computers. When he heard I had one, he bawled me out. "Those sons of bitching computers are no good, I tell ya. One of these days everyone's going to wake up to that." His logic escaped me—his often did. He drove a truck; why couldn't I run a PC? How was his complicated machinery all that different from my complicated machinery?

Dick was just plain scared. His modest shell games with cash and barter couldn't hope to fool the auditing mainframes of the government. And he saw the new generation of lab-coated technicians as an alien race that was subtly displacing him and the other guys from the neighborhood. My becoming one of this bland new race was a kind of treason.

> "Men have become the tools of their tools."
>
> *Henry David Thoreau*[4]

Dick passed on a few years ago, and I hope he has found peace in a computerless heaven, with flirty waitresses and lots of ethnic jokes. But the world is still populated with people troubled by the things that troubled him:

- a world of technology run by experts, often to the detriment of average people who never get with the program;
- a world in which Big Brother is a computer, and no one keeps any secrets from him;
- a world of absolute, indisputable measurements, where a handshake or a wink or a roaring laugh carry no weight at all.

THIS MAGIC MOMENT

Right now is an important moment in computer history. Extraordinarily talented computer scientists have created a world in which almost anything is possible. At the same time, ordinary people are demanding to be part of the action. The two ends of the spectrum analog—As opposed to digital. It is used to describe transmittable information that has not yet been reduced to numerical values (i.e., digitized). The phone is an analog technology because the voice vibrations it transmits are "analogous" to your real voice.

biff—A verb, meaning how your Internet program alerts you to incoming mail. Supposedly derived from the sound dogs make at approaching mail carriers.

are rushing to meet one another: gigaflop geniuses versus the PC peasantry. The geniuses properly belong out on the cusp, coming up with new things, which, being new, are always hard. We peasants benefit from this quest for the new, but mainly in the long term, i.e., when the new has become old.

Short-term, we wish the geniuses would focus on our needs today for simple, easy-to-use machines and programs. While the geniuses push the envelope pursuing things the rest of us can't even hold in our minds, we wish they would focus on incremental improvements to existing tools. They create new worlds; we just want to avoid assigning function keys.

What keeps this unique moment from being a happy one is that we are all of us at war. Technology has embroiled producers and users in a war of nerves. It is not true to say that most technology people are indifferent to the needs of ordinary customers. But some are, and I have an example.

TECHNOPHOBIA

GILLETTE RESIDENT IS ARRESTED AFTER
SHOOTING HIS COMPUTER

A Gillette man was arrested at his home last Thursday night after he fired eight bullets at his home computer, according to police.

The man, Michael A. Case, 35, of 64 Summit Avenue, was arrested shortly after 11 p.m. at his house when police said they received a report that shots were fired. They arrived at the home to find a .44 Magnum automatic handgun and a shot-up IBM personal computer with a Princeton Graphics System monitor.

The monitor screen was blown out by the blasts and its inner workings were visible, Lt. Donald Van Tassel said on Monday. The computer, which had bullet holes in its hardware, was hit four times while four more bullet holes were found in various areas next to the computer, Van Tassel said.

"The only thing he (Case) said was that he was mad at his computer so he shot it," Van Tassel said.

Case was surprised when police arrested him because he didn't think he was breaking the law, Van Tassel said. "He couldn't understand why he couldn't shoot his own computer in his own home," Van Tassel said.[5]

I once knew a man who could not work in an office because he said the noise of the machines—the whir of fans, pulse of the computers, faint hum of fluorescent lights—discombobulated him. He truly believed the machines were malicious spirits, demonic entities conspiring to shatter his serenity. Of course, his smoking an ounce of pot a week probably didn't help matters.

Can machines make us crazy? I'm assured that they can. We can all conjure images of technology fraying our nerves to the breaking point. Smoke and sparks billowing from our hard drive slots. A modem that refuses to dial a number. A 900-page manual that tells everything you want to know about a product except how to make it work.

Techies call anyone who can't hop onto their level of thinking technophobes—a word too often used to mean too many things. Technophobia is what techies call those people who cannot figure out how to use stuff, who neither invest in technology nor try to learn it, or, if forced to learn it, rely exclusively on technical support people instead of reading the documentation or attending conventional training sessions. It sounds like an out for the techno averse—technophobia being a condition we can't help, thus relieving us of responsibility for our actions (and our inactions).

Technophobia, used this way, is a blaming diagnosis, a caricature depicting someone who acts like a deliberate moron around computers. To be honest,

"In a way, staring into a computer screen is like staring into an eclipse. It's brilliant and you don't realize the damage until it's too late."

Bruce Sterling[6]

some of us *are* deliberate morons around computers. On a bad day, we all are. But it's still a pretty mean thing to say about someone.

Every year we read in the paper about some poor soul like Michael Case, who tried for years to do right by the things around him, but who, in a berserk moment of passion, took out his frustrations on his television, or his PC, or a pay phone, with a revolver. The story will elicit our amused sympathy, as we imagine the smoke and static rising out of the stricken machine. We all have felt that way from time to time but had only half the hardware on hand.

Psychologists speak clinically of technophobia as a genuine and sometimes crippling condition, in which the individual is simply unable to deal with machines. Anxiety prevents certain people from performing tasks as simple as dialing the telephone. The condition is treated as other irrational phobias are: victims are asked to describe the worst thing that could happen in an engagement with a computer or telephone or VCR or database. Of course, there really is nothing life-threatening about these things (setting aside the ergonomic problems discussed in a later chapter). The fear is unapologetically irrational.

"My nephew Edward says machines are like dogs. They can sense when you don't like them."

Mary McGrory[7]

The question the rest of us must ask ourselves is, if technology makes us a little crazy, and we don't want to be crazy, exactly how crazy don't we want to be? Because there is a continuum of noncrazy, and each of us needs to select our proper bandwidth within it. First, there's *absolutely not crazy*. Your brain pulses in a pure alpha state, unencumbered by DOS manuals or call waiting. You sleep on the beach and dine on cracked coconuts and conch. Warm breezes caress your toe-hairs. It's doable, if you own the island, and your taxes are prepaid.

Then there's *acceptably crazy*. A little bit of tension is said to aid digestion. Without some tension, we lose our sense of ourselves. Maybe we can pick and choose which hassles we can put up with and which ones we can put behind us.

And there's *unacceptably crazy*, which is how many of us feel now. Confused: We don't know how to make this stuff work, beyond a few basic tricks. Fearful: What if something goes awry when you really need it? Angry: Why didn't they tell us that "100 percent compatible" meant "99.99 percent compatible"? That warranties expire when the company expires? That HIT ANY KEY does not mean finding a key that says ANY?

Technology provokes bipolar human responses, compulsion, and avoidance. Compulsion is *Wow!* It begins as giddy delight and mutates gradually into the behaviors of addiction. Avoidance is *Ack!* It begins as mild resistance to an idea and mutates quickly into mindless denial.

We tend to view the world as divided into these two camps. Those who can and those who cannot. In my view, it would be more accurate to describe each of us this way—as divided into a part that is genuinely curious about technology and another part that runs like a rabbit from it. Each of us has a different mix but each part can get us into trouble.

Neither side is safe ground. We can easily underdo or overdo our attachment to technology. Going whole hog over one thing necessarily means you cannot go even partial hog over something else. On the other hand, to withdraw entirely from a useful technology like networking or multimedia is to hide one's head in the sand. It translates to lost productivity, lost opportunity, lost "currency."

> "I saw the best minds of my generation destroyed by madness."
>
> *Allen Ginsberg*[8]

The two great work technologies—computers and the telephone and all that has sprung from each—have made us more productive, made us "work smarter," allowed us to make more money, and doggone it, they've made our lives more interesting.

Having said all that, technology has not come into our lives without cost, to us as persons, or to us as a society. In what ways has the information age moved us off our better base? We know what we have gained. But what have we lost in the gaining?

THE TEN PARADOXES

The core tenet of this book is that the machines and programs we use to interact with the world of information cause us much unhappiness, frustration, and tension even as they increase our productivity. Those of us who don't "get" technology feel shut out. Those who love it too much feel their lives slipping out of kilter as they mutate into techno droids. And those of us in the middle are just depressed at the high price our technological wonders exact from

> "Guns don't
> kill computers.
> People kill
> computers."
>
> *Eric F.
> Johnson*[9]

us—in money, in learning, in re-learning, in time, in waste, in our health and peace of mind. This book is mostly for this middle group—the "walking wounded" of the working world.

Technology foists a series of miserable paradoxes upon us. Behind every promise it holds out to make our lives easier and happier, it hides a knife it intends to stick in us sooner or later. This book is organized around these paradoxes:

- **The speed of technological progress makes it impossible to catch up.**

Technology races. Chip speeds, storage requirements, product upgrades constantly demand more from users. Speed creates megastress within the technology industry, which is then passed on to us. The result is a footrace nearly everyone loses—users against the industry, people against their machines, nations against nations, all of us against one another.

- **Technology is a common language no two people speak in common.**

Technology generalizes. Industry treats users as if we are all the same, like clone computers. But we are all different, and our differences explain why some of us intuitively "get" technology better than others.

- **Technology inevitably isolates its users.**

Technology confuses. Sure, we have computer networks and e-mail. But those of us who remember the old days remember when a team worked all in one room together. You had lunch together, you gossiped, you blew smoke in one another's face. It was terrible, but it was intimate. We always knew computers turned us into numbers. But until the wall partitions went up, and the passwords were handed out, and the account numbers were assigned, we didn't realize that we were units, as interchangeable as tires. The irony of connectivity—whether through radio, TV, phone, fax, or modem—is that we only connect metaphorically. We never really meet. Because none of us are quite sure what we're talking about when we talk about computers, we tend to talk over our own heads. We nod as if we understand, and maybe we think we do. But we don't.

■ **The more open the architecture, the more you need a third-party repair team.**

Technology breaks. We used to think car repair was bad. Finding a reliable repair party for your PC or phone system is tougher. Few repair centers give customers a clear idea when a repair will be finished or what the cost parameters are. Meanwhile, unless you have a backup system and backed-up, ready-to-use data, you are marooned. You yourself are inoperative. You are broken. You are "down."

■ **The technology-rich get richer, and the rest get buried.**

Technology disappoints. While computers promise productivity advances, the actual experience often comes up short of expectations. You change the way you work from top to bottom—and in the end you aren't making any more money. Worse, if you are an employee and you do succeed in increasing productivity, you may be rewarded by losing your job. If every worker is doing the work of two workers, the organization should require only half as many workers.

> ## WHY COMPUTERS ARE COMPLICATED
>
> First, what a PC does is invisible to the eye. The microscopic pathways of the microprocessor, the light beam of the laser, the electrical stream racing through the system, cannot be observed and thus are difficult to comprehend. A PC is not like a toaster or typewriter, where if you push the button, you see the light go on or the gear turn around.
>
> Second, hardware and software designers are not typical users. Engineers naturally think like engineers, not like nonengineers. They are not interested in the rear guard, where the great mass of us pitch our tents. Their fascination is the avant garde, which they alone can understand. The products they create for one another are wheeled down to us with no love and even less interest.

■ **You can't afford it; you can't afford to be without it.**

Technology costs. All this stuff, analog or digital, is expensive. You save up $2,000 for a good laser printer, but the $2,000 is just the beginning. Every couple of months it will cost you another $200 in cartridges and other supplies. You tell yourself that the productivity increase justifies the expense. But if it does, where are the numbers? Where are the dollars?

■ **That which does not destroy you can still cause major problems.**

Technology maims. Magazine articles list a dozen ways working on a computer can hurt you. You can get carpal tunnel syndrome from a poor keyboard. Eyestrain from quivering monitor images and glare. Backache from bending all day over your machine. Hernias and tendinitis from lugging the ultralite notebook plus printer plus case plus overhead projector through the Dallas–Fort Worth airport. Miscarriages from monitor radiation during pregnancy. Brain tumors from all those happy conversations on the car phone. Maybe none of those things happens to you, but you worry about them anyway. How come they are never mentioned in the ads?

■ **Systems designed to make the world a better place instead place the world in jeopardy.**

Technology despoils. It may seem to be clean and a friend to the earth, but the more we examine technology the more we see it is creating significant toxic-waste and solid-waste problems.

■ **Technology doesn't lie, but it can easily make a liar out of you.**

Technology corrupts. In showing us an easier way, it seduces us into doing everything that way. It tempts us to pretend we are things we are not. It creates veils and masks to hide behind and be different than we are.

■ **That which was supposed to comfort us instead gives us the willies.**

Technology scares. The idyllic future promised by computers threatens to isolate us even more from one another, creating a class of technology haves and have-nots, and foisting new concepts upon us that very few will be able to grasp.

Beyond these paradoxes, computer technology causes other distress, which we will discuss in passing:

■ **It discriminates.** It tends to invalidate age-old skills and traditions while rewarding those with the affinity—and the cash—to embrace the new. It downgrades right-brain (artistic, nuanced) talents and sets the left hemisphere (analytical, binary) high on a pedestal. The infobahn will have several classes for its passengers: first class, coach, and stranded on the shoulder.

■ **It riles.** In yesterday's correspondence, it was rare to write angry letters attacking one another. In cyberspace, however, where we never see our counterpart's eyes, it is commonplace. We lose track of how we come across to people. We are like bombardiers, dropping explosives from a great, safe height. The average newcomer to the Internet (newbie) is welcomed with the same warmth as the first mallard in duck season.

■ **It threatens.** Information is the essence of power. Whoever has information about you has power over you. Whoever has information that you need and don't have has power over you. Despite a great deal of talk about how technology democratizes— e.g., the fax brigades at Tienanmen Square, consumer information sharing on the Internet, Ross Perot's electronic town hall forums—in the meantime it creates a two-tiered society of those who have some technology and those who don't have any.

> "Beyond a shadow of a doubt, it was technology that brought down communism."
>
> *David Hockney*[10]

Put 'em all together, they spell pain, a condition we are going to call techno crazed—a destabilization of the human psyche brought on by little things made of silicon and wires. We know the problem starts in the computer brain. But the cure must come where the pain is greatest—in ours.

COMPUTER WISDOM

We are all a little myopic when it comes to technology. The wisdom of the technophobe is to urge us to repent and forget we ever invented chips, pixels, and interfaces. The wisdom of the techno natural is that technology is power, and the few who master it will also gain mastery over those who can't. The wisdom of the rest of us is that computer technology will have its way with us no matter what, so we may as well brace for the onslaught.

Somewhere between demonization, deification, and despair, there must be a sane approach to computing. Perhaps it goes something like:

> Grant us the serenity to accept the things we cannot change, the courage to change the things we can, and the wisdom to know the difference.

For us to make peace with the machines, we have to figure out our proper relationship with them. This relationship is different for every individual. Some of us will genuinely thrive on a high-technology diet. Others of us will do fine without even a minimum daily allowance of it. The important thing is not to sell ourselves short—to extract from technology the most good that our personalities and attitudes will allow.

Two forces can alleviate techno craziness. The first is the technology industry—the people who develop, make, and sell machines and programs. Generally speaking, they are dedicated to making technology more "people-literate"—able to anticipate and relate to our lifeform. But it is hard for them. First, technology is not easy; making it easy is one of the most complex technological challenges there is. Second, companies naturally seek advantage over one another, and this prevents them from always doing the user-friendly thing, such as making computers that all work alike.

The second and more powerful force is you, the user. Only you know what you want and need. Only you know what you can afford and what your special hang-ups and handicaps are. It's your job to get a good grasp on your personal limitations so you are not sucked into the misery/poverty/desolation that otherwise lie in store for you.

Technology in its happiest moments makes people into gods of the Greco-Roman sort—superhuman in capabilities but retaining our very human nature. The problem is, it has also brought upon us profound frustrations, anxieties, and pain. Instead of making us gods, it has turned us into dogs—our goodwill abused, our loyalties taken for granted.

> "Imagine if every Thursday your shoes exploded if you tied them the usual way. This happens to us all the time with computers, and nobody thinks of complaining."
>
> *Jef Raskin*[11]

Technology is a houseguest that has taken up residence in our lives unbidden. We have the options of welcoming the guest warmly or giving him the cold shoulder. It doesn't matter, because the guest is here to stay no matter what you do, like some crazy, invasive uncle who butts into every conversation. You can shush him all you like, but Uncle Iggy will not go away.

The attainment of techno wisdom requires that each of us walk a personal tightrope between what the market offers and what is best for us. Industry can bend over backwards until it falls over, trying to meet people's needs. But at some point we have to master ourselves and make peace with our machines.

I hope this book equips 98-pound techno weaklings with weapons to help them resist the predations of techno bullies and illuminates a pathway to serenity for the techno obsessed, who have let machines get the better of them. I want it to help you negotiate the tightrope of technology. It explains when it's defensible to be a nut about technology and when it's OK to turn your back on it. Perhaps most important, I want it to help you find your appropriate level of involvement.

One more thing. If you manage to attain wisdom, or a semblance of wisdom, or if all you succeed in doing is becoming a little less techno crazed, just wait a bit. Something new and wonderful is headed your way, and it will make you crazy all over again.

CHAPTER ■ 1

How Speed Hurts Us
And Why We Can't Slow It Down

Being a summary of how technology makes us more powerful, but in the process causes us anxieties our forefathers never dreamed of

Come on. Let's don our virtual history helmets and imagine a composite inventors' exhibition hall circa 1900. Row after row of new and improved inventions are on display, and every few feet visored sales clerks hawk their newfangled wares. An enormous red, white, and blue banner proclaims the theme: "Years of Augmentation."

THE AUGMENTATION BALL

Notice the young men and women—your great-grandfathers and great-grandmothers—rubbernecking at the new machines. How turned on they are by this idea of augmentation. For centuries the world has changed very gradually. By the twentieth century, humans had advanced considerably beyond the scope of their ancestors. A horse, a lever, a pump, a plow all made life easier by making one person the equivalent of perhaps a half dozen persons. That's what our great-grandparents were, augmented by a factor of six. Six-in-oners.

Then, along came the first wave of communications technologies, and the six-in-oners began to augment exponentially. Great Grandpa and Great Grandma sat at a typewriter, or witnessed it in operation, and they intuited the idea of a single individual becoming a virtual publishing company. A dozen-in-one.

They pulled the crank on an adding machine, and the teeth of the gears dug in, and the cams spun, and Great Grandma and Great

SPEED
Paradox #1

The speed of technological progress makes it impossible to catch up.

"My God, it talks!"

Dom Pedro, emperor of Brazil, upon witnessing a telephone in operation, Centennial Exposition, Philadelphia, 1876[1]

Grandpa read the sum and realized that the computer of that day—a human being with an ink pen, perched on a high stool, bending over a ledger book—was instantly obsolete. A machine could do the work of a score of Bob Cratchits—twenty-in-one!

They watched a telegrapher tap out a message to some distant destination and get a reply within moments. Or they listened to the crackle of a wireless transmission, emanating from some mysterious point, many cities away.

They could have studied any of the other technologies that developed into today's computer office hardware—Edison's tape recorder, which paved the way for today's data storage systems, or the cathode ray tube, which evolved into today's TVs and monitors.

The communications age our grandparents saw dawning has wound down, replaced by our own age of information systems and networks. We sit in our offices and homes surrounded by the machines, engulfed in an ocean of electrons that mean things. Fax machines, personal computers, modems, fiber optics and ISDN pathways, the information superhighway.

What we are is enhanced and exponentiated; in a word, augmented. Douglas Engelbart, revered today as "the father of the graphical user interface," used that word when he predicted in 1963 what today's Macintosh and Windows computers would be like, in a famous essay titled "A Conceptual Framework for the Augmentation of Man's Intellect."[2] He was the first person to think of the computer as a tool every individual could use that would multiply that individual's abilities to think and learn.

The old world was a place of varied things. The new world, augmented by computers, is by and large a place of numbers. We have assigned numbers to everything, so that everything can be represented on the screen, almost real. Pixels representing actual brushstrokes are numbers. A poem of heartfelt emotion is a series of coded hexadecimals in a word processing program. A printout of a brain scan, showing what you are, inside where you think, is just a shifting array of zeroes and ones, ons and offs.

The numeralization or digitization of the world is the source of our augmented powers. If the worker of two generations ago was a six-in-oner, what is the worker of the information age? The worker fills a dozen different functions without breaking a sweat—serving as one's own typist, accountant, tax preparer, librarian, file clerk, purchasing agent. Moreover, the worker is linked by a dotted line to the accumulated knowledge of millions of people.

> "Life was simple before World War II. After that, we had systems."
>
> *Grace Hopper*[3]

When the ornate latticework of the information network is finally laid over top of us, each of us will be augmented to stratospheric levels—a million-in-one and better.

We are still far from being fully augmented. Every day we add new power, because every day the technology available to us becomes more powerful.

Computers have advanced to the point where they can exponentiate themselves. Every month some new speed barrier falls—millions of instructions per second (mips), billions per second (gigaflops), trillions (teraflops), bytes per second (bps), a million cycles per second (megahertz or MHz) and so forth. No one dares put a limit on future possibilities, including computers made of single molecules, and single atoms, operating at the speed of light.

Computer technology is electronic. It is driven by electrons, with the theoretical capability of coursing at superconductive speeds—the speed of light, 186,000 miles per second. Even slowed down by copper wire, electricity isn't something you want to get into a footrace with.

> "Technology is a queer thing. It brings you great gifts with one hand, and it stabs you in the back with the other."
>
> *C.P. Snow*[4]

Then consider the cornerstone of today's office technology, the microchip. A processor chip is essentially a maze, similar to those Cracker Jack prize games in which you try to get the ball bearings to follow the pathway to the holes punched in the cardboard. Only the ball bearings are electrons, and the pathways within the puzzle are made of logic—yes, no, if, then. All these decisions are made at speeds that even in the first primitive chips were described as blinding. Blinding is probably not the best adjective, considering that the process is invisible, but it stuck, and we are stuck with it.

Chips keep getting faster. Moore's Law states that the power of microprocessor chips doubles every eighteen months, with no increase in cost. In the actual marketplace Moore's Law is close to holding true:

Intel chips	Released	Clock speed (MHz)
8088	1978	4.77–10
80286	1984	6–20
80386	1986	16–33
80486	1989	25–66
Pentium	1993	40–100

So you have an economy in which the core item doubles in power and speed about every year and a half. Imagine any other industry absorbing such revolutionary advances with such rapidity. An auto whose basic engine can attain 100 miles per hour in year one, would easily cruise at 7,000 miles per hour within ten years. Today's washing machine would whisk every vestige of grime from your clothes in 30 seconds. Each match in a book would have the throw-weight of a quarter stick of dynamite.

Furthermore, the ratcheting up of machine speed appears unstoppable. As it speeds up, everything else speeds up with it. It changes everything about life—the way we work, the way we plan, the way we think. Few of us appreciate the quantum nature of this acceleration, in particular the downside of things happening so fast.

What Speed Does to the Industry

Speed is the archenemy of serenity. It is stress in italics.

OK, you say, exactly how does the speed of some doodad inside a computer affect my life? Besides, speed is nice, on roller coasters, or if you are late for a meeting 20 miles away. Speed gets things done faster so you have more time to (yawn, stretch) kick back. How does Moore's Law, a yardstick for the computer industry, not me, stand between me and my bliss?

Obviously, computer technology enhances our lives in many ways, and few of us, even recounting the negative aspects of computers, want to go back to the unaugmented days of toil and repetition. But the negatives must still be taken into account. What follows is a top-down depiction of how the stress and tension jam-packed into a microprocessor makes its way from the clean room to your room and finally into your psyche.

> "Computers can figure out all kinds of problems, except the things in the world that just don't add up."
>
> *James Magary*[5]

First of all, *chip speed keeps the computer industry on a short, tight leash.* If an entire industrial community survives by making software or peripherals that run on, say, an Intel Pentium chip, then that community has a short lifetime in which to develop products that work with the emerging chip. To make matters even more frantic, hardware technology is driven by a software counterpart—computer operating systems. You want to have your product designed, debugged, manufactured, shrink-wrapped and on the shelves while OS2/Warp or Windows 95 or System 7.2 is still current. It's an excruciatingly narrow horizon, and it quickly gobbles up any venture cash that a small start-up company has managed to set aside. There are no second chances—you come in first in the sprint, or you lose. Software developers tear their hair out at these time constraints. The market is extremely unforgiving when products are released prematurely. Yet the task of properly compiling a major software application is inescapably laborious and time-consuming.

3000 BC. The abacus, invented in Babylon and found nearly everywhere. The ultimate in ease of use. Just after World War II, a clerk from China won a refereed calculating competition against a sergeant in the U.S. army equipped with the latest electromechanical computer.

2800 BC. Stonehenge, on England's Salisbury Plain. Twenty miles across in its entirety, this arrangement of stones and geoforms served as an analogical cosmic clock. It is the first plain-top computer.

1800 BC. The Aztecs and Maya discover zero. Arab scholars also begin working with the concept at about this time. You can't have a binary system without zero.

> "Computers are useless. They can only give you answers."
>
> *Pablo Picasso*[6]

KEY INFORMATION TECHNOLOGIES

There is a tendency to equate information technology with computers. As we sink deeper into the era of interactivity, networking, multimedia, and the information superhighway, it becomes apparent that the individual PC is just a switching system for a host of other technologies, most of which started out as analog devices—electronic analogies to reality—but are now mutating into true digital devices whose data can be manipulated by computers. Here is an incomplete list of the most basic technologies that plug into your desktop world:

Alternating current
Mechanical switches
Vacuum tube switches
Transistor switches
Integrated circuits
Silicon chip switches
Microprocessors
Core memory
Batteries
Cathode ray tube (monitors)
Magnetic media (recording tape, floppy disks)
Laser media (compact disks)

(Continued on page 23)

Sales and marketing people look at the calendar and swallow hard. If their product reaches the market a month after a competing product from Microsoft or Borland, it will have to be twice as good to win favor, and even then magazine editors are likely to yawn and say, "But we just did a word processor cover article in January."

Speed undermines quality assurance. If you have a narrow window of opportunity to exploit (a twelve-month development cycle) and a narrower market window (ten months of shelf life before the next model supersedes yours), you have to move fast, and that means cutting corners. New computer products are more likely to fail in some way than just about any other appliance or electronic gadget you can buy. Why? Because the best companies have the hardest time meeting demand. To get the product out the door, or to make a profit on a narrow margin, compromises are made, and the products are either malconfigured or include a bad part. An hour after repacking and plugging in, you're on the phone, and the heel print of betrayal and disappointment is visible upon your countenance.

Speed destroys the best and brightest of our talent, and they disappear forever. No industry attracts such talented people, and then burns them out more quickly and more irremediably, than information technology. And those whom technology does not destroy it distracts. Think how much happier a place the world would be if, instead of making machines that make us break down periodically in tears, these bright stars had dedicated their talents to curing diseases, ending warfare, plugging the ozone hole. We know we gained tiny processors, but we'll never know what we lost. (Then again, at least they didn't go into investment banking.)

Speed bloats inventories. When product lines change drastically every 90 days, inventories back up, once-new devices become commodity materials, value plummets, and pieces are either sold off at sharp discounts or junked. Think of all the IBM AT and Apple Mac SE boxes, ready to ship, that never shipped.

Speed takes an agonizing toll on investors. Because time is short, margins are thin. Makers of clones dare not set prices a single percentage point higher than their competitors. Yet that percentage point may be the difference between profitability and ruination. Last year's price champs are nearly always this year's also-rans. Some other company always comes along with a way to deliver the goods to customers faster and cheaper.

No industry has ever yielded the kind of megabang ringups that computer technology has. And no industry has left its dead strewn about in such numbers. Failed companies by the thousands dot the techno graveyard.

Analog image production (camera)
Analog wire transmission (telegraphy)
Analog voice transmission (telephony)
Analog text production (typewriter)
Wireless signal transmission (wireless telegraphy)
Wireless audio transmission (radio)
Wireless audio/visual transmission (television)
Wireless analog transmission (cellular telephony)
Wireless digital transmission (radio modems)
Radio data transmission (ticker tape)
Analog sound recording (audio records and tapes)
Analog audio/visual recording (video tapes)
Digital telephony
Digital text production (phototypesetting)
Digital audio/visual transmission (high density television)
Digital sound recording (compact disks and DAT)
Wired audiovisual transmission (cable, closed-circuit)
Analog Text Transmission (teletype)
Analog image transmission (facsimile)
Digital image transmission (faxmodem)
Modem transmission
On-line services
The Internet

SEVEN BASIC MOVIE PLOTS ABOUT TECHNOLOGY[7]

Hollywood has figured out only a handful of ways to put computers into stories. To save you money on future science fiction movies, here are all the plots there ever will be:

"John Henry was a steel drivin' man, lord, lord."

Plot pits a good old muscle-and-blood human being against a machine. The machine wins on quantity, but the human wins on quality. Tracy and Hepburn pioneered this plotline with *Desk Set*.

"How to serve man."

We think technology is our friend, until we see what it keeps in the refrigerator. The telescreens in *1984*, the unstoppable nuclear devices in *Fail Safe* and *Dr. Strangelove*, and the techno-tyranny of Woody Allen's *Sleeper* all qualify.

"A child shall save them."

Technology is too wonderful for computer professionals to

(Continued on page 25)

WHAT SPEED DOES TO US

That's what speed has done to the information industry itself—made it crazy and left it gibbering through broken teeth. And it's doing the same thing to us, only worse, because we are at the end of the whipcrack.

Speed forces upon us a learning curve that never lets up. No sooner do you learn one tool, you must learn another, or its upgrade. What other products require you to climb the face of El Capitán before you can derive benefit from them? Computers are not like cars or televisions. By the time you master your current toy, a big chunk of its productive lifetime is gone.

Speed robs us of reflection. In the old days, writing something important meant writing three separate drafts, each one from scratch. Writing took time and labor, but more than that it required thought and a sense of purpose. The "second draft" on a modern word processor is a quick layover, and the "third draft" is just a touch-up. The sense of deeper, calmer purpose has been whisked away with the ease of electronic rewriting.

Speed dims our eye toward "individuation." Before we technologize we live in a custom world in which every object is unique. A letter to grandma is a letter to grandma alone. After we technologize we start looking for short cuts. Form letters with boilerplate inserts. Preprinted labels instead of handwritten envelopes. As speed picks up, the quality of our output—the deep design, not the outward gloss—gets shoddier and shoddier. Computers turn perfectly good people into purveyors of mass-produced goods—into factories or McDonalds.

Speed imposes its own capricious modes of thinking upon us. Where we once thought our own thoughts in our own way, we now, unconsciously, call up our own mental files, examine or alter them, and save them again. Society shares a Microsoft Windows interface. Our minds have mice. The benefit of this universal interface is that, like driving on the expressway, we all have another civilized way to behave and interact with one another. The minus is that we all slip into the rut of Microsoft mind—just when we need to plow fresh furrows.

Speed clear-cuts our forest of opportunity. Technology has decimated entire livelihoods (typists, bookkeepers, order fillers, draftsmen) and pried others (accounting, publishing, printing, engineering) away from their core competencies. When we think of what we do with our computers, the word we choose is seldom craftsmanship. In olden

mess with. Only kids can really fathom its mysteries. *D.A.R.R.Y. L., War Games, E.T.*

"Nothing can go worng."

The machine that was supposed to be so infallible goes nuts and kills everyone. *HAL 2000, War Games, Westworld.*

"Half man, half machine."

Machines with human personalities, or people who bond with machines. From Robbie the Robot to Johnny 5 to R2D2, from *Commander Data* to *The Terminator*, it holds perpetual appeal.

"The friends you keep."

Do evil geniuses have all the really good computers, or does it just seem that way? Lex Luthor is the archetypal computer criminal.

"Lost in cyberspace."

People disappear into cyberspace (*Jumping Jack Flash*), virtual reality (*Lawnmower Man*), or are shrunk down to the size of pulsing electrons (*Tron, Fantastic Journey*).

days you learned a trade and practiced it for life. Not anymore. The information upheaval is displacing people like, well, like nobody's business. Experts say the worker of the next generation will change careers a half dozen times—not out of choice but necessity. If we never labor long at a single skill, will we ever get good at anything? With

bitstream—There is a famous font company called Bitstream, and it sounds like something an advertising firm would pick for a name. But the word actually goes back to the early computer pioneers in England during World War II. The Collossus computer was programmed by punched paper tape. But the tape was always breaking, which caused costly shutdowns. Computer scientist Thomas Flowers decided to get rid of the tapes altogether, by generating electronic pulses within the computing machine, to replace the tapes. These electronic pulses were dubbed the bit-stream, from the word bit, which meant binary digit. This bitstream generator eliminated both tape setup time and tape breakage downtime. It was one of the first uses of vacuum tubes in a computer, which was very controversial at that time. The special bitstream vacuum tubes also had an interesting name—*thyratons.*

black hole—Where e-mail goes when it doesn't go where it's supposed to go. Alternatively, computer-aware astronomers suspect black holes in the cosmos are where God is dividing by zero. See *divide by zero.*

machines, will we ever need to? The focus of personal pride shifts from, Did I do my very best? to Did I make deadline?

Speed makes it impossible to plan. Instant communication raises expectations of instant results. It puts everything in the evanescent now. Despite everything the computer press tells us about how computers free us to use our intelligence, how many of us feel freed? And how free is free—free to do 200 hours of production in a 50-hour week? If everyone uses information technology, information technology ceases to be a competitive advantage. The net result is that everyone is running the race at 150 miles per hour.

Speed sullies our thrift ethic. Why shop for bargains (used, outdated, liquidated technology) when new technology is almost as cheap as old? Remember in *The Empire Strikes Back* how heedlessly that hippo-headed botwright worker knocked off C3PO's head? No one really fixes computers any more— they just replace whole modules and throw the nonworking one away. It's too expensive to try to save anything. Sweep it into the dustbin and start fresh with new items.

Speed has fixed us forever with solid-waste headaches. When the life cycle of a computer chip is only eighteen months, the turnover is terrific. At this moment some 75 million personal computers are in consumers' homes and offices. But we know that more than half of these are nearing the paperweight stage of usefulness—they are too limited and too slow to be of value. Within five years nearly all 75 million will be deemed obsolete, and 20 million replacements will have sprung into existence. Result: a mountain range of tangled wire, metal, plastic, and glass—a solid-waste nightmare, a smoldering reproach to our lust for high speeds.

CHAPTER ■ 2

Why We Don't "Get" Technology And Whose Fault That Is, and What Can Be Done About It

In which the author bemoans the gulf of misunderstanding betwixt technology makers and technology users and fashions a curious new paradigm for users taking the bull by the horns

I just this moment logged off the Internet. I was visiting a Usenet newsgroup room called alt.folkore.computers. This is a newsgroup made up almost entirely of workers in the technology field— software programmers, development professionals, hardware engineers, and technical support people. It is the same group where I encountered the fellow who went ballistic and said that one day "Mike Finley" would be a catchphrase for a total loser.

I went there to ask the following question: Are technology products on today's store shelves too hard to learn? I expected a few people to concede the point that, yes, documentation tends to be boring and incomplete and yes, products are sometimes designed without much consideration for the people who will eventually use them. But that's not what I got. Instead I got anger. And frustration.

"Users are lazy beyond belief," one tech support staff person wrote me. "We give them manuals. We give them help files they can use while they are operating the program. We give them a free 800 number where they can find technical support for 90 days. We provide support forums on CompuServe and America Online where we answer their questions free of charge.

"But many users steadfastly refuse to crack open a manual. They refuse to look at what the help files say. When we explain what they're doing wrong on the phone, or in a forum, they whine that it's too difficult, and why do we make things so hard for them."

A software engineer put it even more bluntly. "You wouldn't operate a car without learning how to drive, but people think computers should just boot up and do what they want. People are trusting their entire businesses, their livelihoods, the livelihood of everyone who works there, to machines they are too lazy to familiarize themselves with."

> ## STALEMATE
> ### Paradox #2
> Computers will always be at odds with human individuality.

"Engineers have long understood that nothing can be foolproof," the engineer told me, "since fools are always so damn clever. Programmers go to great lengths to ensure they've taken care of every possible error condition. But such efforts are almost entirely in vain, since there is always a complete dolt out there who will exceed their estimates of the lowest common fool."

This gentleman had undoubtedly suffered greatly at the hands of a long stream of anxious, whining users in crisis. He had arrived at a state of zero tolerance for the very people who put bread on his table. I wanted to grab him by his virtual lapels and coax him toward a more forbearing position. Surely some users were lazy, manipulative knuckleheads, I conceded. But surely there were many who were trying their best but just not "getting it"? Perhaps even, as customers, it was their right to demand usable technology. It wasn't as if companies weren't billing the products as user-friendly, easy to learn, etc. Buyers buy stuff because sellers recommend it.

"Mary had a little RAM, maybe a meg or so."

Unknown

But I got nowhere. His worldview was set. Users were a breed of demons, put on earth to torment him with idiot questions. And I would guess that, with his attitude, users on the other end felt pretty much the same about him.

WHO IS TECHNOLOGY FOR?

A good philosophical framework for discussing customer relationships is quality. Quality is a big topic, and people disagree on what it is. In our time, two passionate quality gurus have battled to define what quality is. Joseph Juran defined quality succinctly as "fitness for use."

> **bogosity**—The measure of a thing's bogusness, falseness or unacceptability.
>
> **bolt-on**—A homemade addendum, usually eccentric in design, to a common product. It works for you, but wait till you are gone and the next person tries to make it work.
>
> **bozotic**—Clownishly bad, as said by programmers of poor programming.

Wm. Edwards Deming defined quality several ways, but in his final book arrived at his simplest summation: "It is something that helps somebody."[1]

Too often, technology companies have applied an inside-out interpretation of Juran's definition. A product is for use when the maker of the product decides it is fit for use. Silicon Valley companies can certainly congratulate themselves for putting out "quality products" from their own expert points of view. American hardware and software is the best in the world, by industry standards. The best minds they could assign to the task stayed up nights thinking what features to pack into their systems and how best to document those features. The result has been products that cheerfully bill themselves as user-friendly and come with a stack of manuals that lead users step by step through the features.

These manuals are written toward a "targeted user" profile. If the product is difficult and advanced in nature, the targeted user will be a power user, someone who can handle any techno task thrown his or her way. If the product seeks a popular audience, the targeted user is someone lower on the evolutionary scale—people intelligent enough and willing enough to teach themselves how the product works.

> "Technology has brought meaning to the lives of many technicians."
>
> *Ed Bluestone*[2]

But this is a shallow and self-serving model. Excellence in materials, assembly, and documentation is great, but it is no guarantee that customers will understand the product. Quality is not a silver bullet to shoot customers with. It should be a banquet to invite customers to join. But with computer technology, it has always been the bullet.

Deming's definition is subtler and deeper and it lends itself to an outside-in approach. A good product by this standard must not only be usable, as defined by the maker, but it must be successfully used, as defined by the user. In the end it must make the customer happy. Like the tree falling in the wilderness, quality must be experienced in order for it to exist.

In the broader Demingite sense, quality reflects a company's understanding of what customers need and a willingness to meet those needs. Quality "occurs" when the things we buy please us. When we are glad we bought them.

For all the intellect and precision that are built into machines and programs, they still frustrate the bejeezus out of most of us. So we have to ask if the deeper aspect of quality is occurring. Do the makers of machines know who we are and what we want? Do they care?

If we users are all the same person, then it doesn't matter what our individual names are. If we're all different, then those who would sell to us had better figure out who we are and what we want from them.

> "The beauty of mechanical problems is that they are often visible to the naked and untrained eye. If white smoke is rising from a disk drive, that is probably where the problem lies, unless your disk drive has just elected the new Pope."
>
> *John Bear*[3]

SUPPOSEDLY THERE ARE ONLY TWO TYPES OF USERS . . .

In the industry view, there are two kinds of people. Their favorites are their targeted customers—power users and willing learners. But in order to sell enough product to make a profit, companies hope to sell to nontargeted people, too. The laggards and technophobes. Us.

We laggards are a little dim about anything new, slow to pick up on things that power users would instantly hail as "intuitive." We are the whiners, bellyaching as we're hauled into the future by our mouse cords. We are the counter-intuitive.

Not to put too fine a point on it, but the first group is smart and the second group is dumb. And it is the view of many techies that the dumb, because they are the buying public, are running the show, and this is terribly, terribly wrong. If a technology company springs a brilliant new product on the market and the dumb portion of the public blinks uncomprehendingly at it, the company blames us dumbbells for not having the requisite number of brain cells to appreciate the high quality that their product represents.

Hogwash

What if the answer is more complicated than smart versus dumb, technophiles versus technophobes?

What if products are wreaking havoc right and left because they are all being designed, manufactured, and taught for one or two kinds of users—very smart, as in the case of advanced CAD systems, and pretty smart, as in the case of metaphor-based operating systems like Windows 95—when there are really many different kinds of users?

I have been working for several years now with one very diverse corporate team of nine people. Our job has been to promote a leading brand of client-server accounting software. Our team of nine works on PCs and communicates via phone, meetings, e-mail, and fax. When I squint, and make a few mental generalizations, I can envision each of these nine people as a distinct personality type, with a different outlook on technology.

Let me describe the members of the team to you, one by one. I'll sand the rough edges on a couple of their personalities to fit them into the nine types. But the types are there—these people really are distinct in the ways I describe. You tell me if these people don't sound more or less like the sorts of people you work with.

■ **Leon** is a *techno natural.* Leon's system is the most advanced in the whole company, not just on our team. He has two gigabytes of hard disk all his own, and he works every byte of it. Leon has a naturally analytical mind, very practical and linear, yet he seems to experience real joy playing with his toys. He is so good at this stuff he seldom needs to refer to manuals or help files. He knows about hidden features. If he's puzzled about something he consults the professional literature or one of the Internet techie newsgroups. He is a perfectionist about technology, the sort of person everyone else with a problem comes to, never guessing the barely concealed contempt he feels for their lack of commitment. He would qualify as a nerd if he didn't have this great, loud laugh. He enjoys being in the spotlight as the team's technology guru. But I think it also makes him anxious, because he is smart enough to know he doesn't really know that much. His fear is that he will diagnose someone else's problem incorrectly, and his reputation will take a hit. He does not want us techno dweebs second-guessing him.

- **Jane** is an *earnest user*, the kind technology companies wish there were more of. She is serious about using computers, networks, and phone technologies as tools to do her work. She reads the manual. She joins user groups. She subscribes to magazines. But she never feels she is making creative sparks with technology. It is just there, plain vanilla, and she succeeds in getting it to do what she requires, period. She is a methodical, diligent thinker whose opinions are respected by the group—not because they are flashy, but because we know she came by them the old-fashioned way, by the sweat of her brow. She is a good analyst, because she is careful and fair-minded. She wishes she could be the sort that could paint outside the lines just once, but it doesn't seem to be in her. She has the healthiest plants of anyone on the team. She keeps a cactus on her typing table that must be two feet high.

- **Edward** is a *people person*. If you need someone to listen to you, to be interested, to take your side, Edward is the guy. His problem with technology is that it is entirely systematic in nature, and he isn't; he has no gift for understanding systems. He does not go around cursing machines, but he avoids them, feeling defeated in advance. Systems are too linear, too mathematical, too logical in nature. If Edward had his druthers, all team problems would be solved by a show of hands, and all substantive business conducted over lunch. What everyone else wants, that's what he wants, too. Computers don't mesh with his organic value system at all. They don't laugh, they don't cry, and if you prick them, they don't bleed. If they just had emotions he might have a chance with them. But they don't, and he doesn't.

- **Clarice** is a *plugger*, no whiz at technology, but skilled at learning a few things, mastering them, and knowing which to try, and when. She is not against reading a manual if it will get her where she needs to go. But she is really only interested in the work itself. She has no real interest in the machines. They are a means to an end, period. She is not willing to spend a lot of valuable time learning them. Her dream technology is a turnkey system that needs no configuring and has all the commands up front where she can see them. To tell the truth, Clarice is not the most exciting person on the team by a long shot. She has been remodeling her home ever since we have known her, and it is all we can do to keep from falling into cataplectic slumber when she brings the subject up. But she is the straightest shooter and hardest worker we have. She never complains about her work, market research, even though it would send most of us packing. She has a disarming sense of humor the rest of us wish were not quite so self-deprecating. She makes the rest of us look better than we are. She takes the work very seriously, and that keeps the rest of us from flying away like lint.

■ **Erroll** is the *quintessential quester*, self-involved, self-directed, impetuous, and constitutionally unable to march in step with any external force, including computer technology. His approach to his responsibilities might best be described as episodic. He has ideas that strike other team members as brilliant—but they have to flesh them out for him. You might say he knows just enough to be dangerous. He knows a few computer basics—how to install a program, how to open a file, and how to import data. After that, he relies shamelessly on nearby office gurus to do the simplest tasks. It might have been his idea to use a software package he saw in an ad, because he was transfixed by what it seemed to promise—but he could never get it to keep those promises back at the office. It isn't his fault he is this way—he has other fish to fry. He is an "artist" at heart, even though he doesn't do any art. It is natural for him to be self-involved to a degree other people can't comprehend, much less sympathize with. He is the type of person tech support professionals tell tall tales about. "You think you talked to an idiot on the phone—wait'll you hear about my guy." But the rest of us like him, because he is fun to be around—and he is a superb copywriter.

> "We were taken to a fast-food cafe where our order was fed into a computer. Our hamburgers, made from the flesh of chemically impregnated cattle, had been boiled over counterfeit charcoal, placed between slices of artificially flavored cardboard and served to us by recycled juvenile delinquents."
>
> *Jean-Michel Chapereau*[4]

■ **Mark** is a *worrier*. His mind is riveted to the negative side of things. He is afraid of things going wrong and he avoids any act that entails what he considers unnecessary risk. He worries about power surges, lightning strikes, file corruption, hitting the wrong key. He sees computers and other technology as fragile. His spirit of caution is a shield against attack from outside forces. He makes multiple backups, keeps his office impeccably clean, and studies the literature for practices causing the least wear and tear on his equipment. For his birthday, we got him a cake with Alfred E. Neuman on it, asking "What, me worry?" He smiled thinly. His definition of technological success—zero mishaps. He is perfectly competent, but unsuited to high-risk assignments, such as lion-taming or new product development. He jokes that he is neurotic but he is really just being careful. Careful is good—Mark is our project treasurer.

- **Aloysius** is a *dreamer*. He lives in the structures he builds to do his work. He was born in Alexandria, Egypt, but he would seem exotic if he was from Keokuk. His actual work never wins awards, but the rest of us marvel at his knack for fashioning menus, batch files, network connections, fax logs, interesting directory patterns, and meticulous maintenance schedules. He is a passionate believer in technology and thinks it holds the answer to reducing the toil and boredom in people's lives. He loves the gee-whiz of technology and has an armload of futuristic books on his credenza. But he just doesn't understand the nuts and bolts of why electronic things work and why they sometimes don't. Always—that's his nickname on the team—is often disappointed that the products he buys don't satisfy the requirements he has created in his head. He keeps tripping over his own high hopes, but he keeps coming back, gamely. We sort of feel protective about Always.

- **Johanna** is a *skeptic*. She comes to the technology table with a good-sized chip already in place on her shoulder. She is impatient when things don't go her way and downright intolerant of steep learning curves. A couple of us call her J-bomb behind her back, because she has great energy but kind of a short fuse. She expects a decently designed software tool to be self-explanatory, useful, and profitable within minutes of breaking the shrinkwrap. She expects things to work, to be understandable, and executable. When they are not, she hurls herself against whatever disappoints her with terrible ferocity. Sometimes Johanna balks at trying new things, lest they fail as badly as the last "improvement" foisted upon us by management. She is intelligent, she is not anti-technology, *but* she is a hothead when things don't go well right away. She expects to be in charge of whatever new gadget she decides to employ and is irritable when they do not immediately yield up their secrets. Johanna can be a real pain at times, but she is valuable to the team because she keeps the rest of us on task. My theory is that since Johanna was the oldest of six kids and spent her teen years baby-sitting everybody, she now treasures her own time. She explained it to me very differently, over cheeseburgers, that her irritability stems from loyalty. She hates to see anyone's time wasted, especially the team's.

■ **Bret** is a *classic technophobe*—all out, no kidding, nothing held back. It's not just that he has no knack for it; he thinks it is bad, the spawn of Satan. Think of him as a computer curmudgeon. He doesn't wear a physical bow tie, but we suspect his soul wears one. He is a dyed-in-the-wool traditionalist. Decades ago he had a poem published in *The Sewanee Review*, and he carries a crumbled tearsheet of it in his wallet, which he takes out with trembling, pathetic hands and shows people. He genuinely reveres the past and wishes he could turn his back on everything modern and go back to the way things used to be. He is not the cleverest person on the team, because there are some ideas he simply will not entertain. But his work is always classy and gives the rest of us a posh veneer. Next to him, we are plastic and he is teak. He is always growling that the team is doing things on computers that could be done just as easily with a pencil and paper. (He is right, but not very often.) He takes his lack of felicity with machines and converts it into feelings of superiority. It is because he is well-rounded and three-dimensional, he says, whereas they are simply high-speed binary idiots. We like having Bret around because he makes us feel hipper than we are.

> "Is electronic corn-on-the-cob really a good idea?"
>
> *Watney's Red Barrel*[5]

That's my team—one of them, anyway. What I would like to propose is that they are your team, too. That is to say, the nine types are a fair breakdown of all the people you work with. Each character represents an elemental attitude about technology. Everyone knows a Johanna, Erroll, and Bret. In fact, everyone at various times, is a Johanna, Erroll, and Bret. No one is a pure techno natural or a pure technophobe—we are all composites of all of these inclinations.[6] But some of our inclinations are dominant in deciding our everyday behavior. On balance, we are more of an Always than a Mark.

What's important is that we agree that in a world where only one or two types of users, techno naturals like Leon and earnest learners like Jane, are being systematically addressed, there are other types of users—billions, maybe—whose peculiar needs are never acknowledged.

OTHER WAYS WE DIFFER

It gets worse. Different users have different physical limitations. We have different IQs. We have multiple intelligences—some of us learn well by rote; some need human interaction; some of us need to have our imaginations engaged; some need military music playing. People have different language orientations. These dimensions of us don't define who we are, but they sure affect our ability to get the most from off-the-shelf technology.

1700 BC. Royal accountants in the court of Akkad keep tallies on clay tablets. The first ceramic data storage device.

356 BC. Aristotle, in an off-the-cuff remark, says, "A thing cannot both be A and not be A." In one remark he encapsulates the core truth of both digital mathematical and logical functions. People hearing him grunt and help themselves to second helpings of dolmati.

65 BC. Archimedes creates his "planetarium"—a geared representation of the sun, moon, and five planets.

1000 AD. The astrolabe, invaluable to navigators, scientists, and astrologers alike.

Whether we admit it or not, we also have different philosophies about technology. Philosophies cut across our user "types." Our types describe who we are as users—who we can't really help being. Our philosophy is the attitude or approach that we adopt. Our philosophies change a lot as we get older and wiser, or even from situation to situation. Our types don't change nearly as much.

People tend to have one of three primary philosophies about technology:

- The *dismals*. These are the users who never asked to be born, and never asked to be shown how a PC works, either. They believe the world is heading inevitably toward a sad end, and that technology, far from saving us from the rapid deterioration waiting just down the pike, is accelerating and exacerbating it. If they could reinvent the world, it might be a kind of Eden in which we have no PCs and no phone banks, and no fig leaves, either. A really dedicated dismal will be dismal about even that idyllic possibility—he will fixate on the pleasures of appendicitis in Paradise.

■ The *hopefuls*. These are the menschen of the computer world. The future as they see it is a mixed bag of good and bad. Technology is surely responsible for making some situations worse, rather than better. On balance, however, technology is here to stay, so why not make the best of it and hope technology can fix itself in time? Maybe suffering through confusing systems and Taiwanian instruction manuals is all part of the suffering in this life that leads to redemption in the next. Or maybe not, but what can you do?

■ The *rhapsodists*. These are the people who design and create systems, and also the people who rush out to buy whatever is new and fall profoundly in love with it until something newer comes along. They have the dream, and they have it bad. They still like nuclear power, even after Chernobyl confirmed the worst suspicion of dismals that our friend the atom was a psychopathic maniac. But rhapsodism is no less honest than the other philosophies; it simply arrives at different conclusions from the available evidence. And give rhapsodists their due—they throw themselves at technology with such positivism that it tends to work a whole lot better for them than it does for the rest of us.

> "I'm pink,
> therefore I'm
> Spam."
>
> *Internet*
> *graffito*

What Industry Can Do

Where all this is leading is a paradox pitting technology against human nature. Technology in the 1990s certainly looks "advanced." Our microchips and networks can turn a head-scratching bumpkin into a sophisticated army of function-completers. But the communication systems that support these technologies (books, videos, training seminars, etc.) are still pretty primitive given the complexity of the communication task they need to perform.

The industries that serve up technology must come to terms with the polymorphous perversity of their clientele. This means conceding that there is a world of legitimate users beyond Leon and Jane, and that their needs deserve to be addressed as much as Leon's and Jane's do.

One way is through multimedia. Instead of, or in addition to, bundling five pounds of books with a software package, or a phone system, or a sound card, why don't manufacturers create interactive audio-video training regimens on CD-ROM? As the software is installed, users are told they may not use the program until they spend a few minutes with the CD-ROM. The CD-ROM will begin with a questionnaire that elicits what the individual user's experience level, personality, tastes, and philosophy are. There is no reason it cannot be presented in multimedia fashion, with appropriate music, animation, and voiceover.

> "Computers are not intelligent. They only think they are."
>
> *Anonymous*

Let's say you have answered the questions. Now the PC takes your answers, digests them, shuffles them all together, and starts to assemble a pathway through a CD-ROM training course that will work especially well for you. Within 60 seconds, the computer has created a custom training package:

Level: Basic. Every detail is explained. Every phrase is defined. Every screen gives you the option of defining any terms used in the presentation by highlighting it with your mouse and clicking. Every question is answered with a speaking voice and an on-screen animation:

> What is Windows? Good question. Windows is a way of computing that uses pictures instead of letters and numbers. Before Windows, computers all had the same screen—24 lines deep and 80 characters across. In Windows, everything is a picture. That means letters and numbers can be any size you want, and screens can include pictures. Instead of typing in difficult commands like DEL C:\LTR\INVOICE*.DOC, Windows lets you give commands by clicking your mouse on a little picture, called an icon. This icon is used for deleting a file. Here is a list of your files. All you have to do to delete a file is touch the file name with the mouse, click it, then click the delete button next to it. See, the file is gone forever.

Narrator: Candace Bergen.

Theme song: Frank Zappa and the Mothers of Invention, performing "Who Are the Brain Police?"

Video montage: John Glenn's triumphal ticker tape trip down Wall Street, segueing into Gerald Ford toasting bread, and the Andy Warhol Rolling Stones album cover.

Other: Since you indicated that your great concern about computing was the fear of ruining something, the CD-ROM bolsters its presentation with periodic assurances that nothing you can do, short of driving over a cliff with the PC strapped to the hood, is likely to damage the machine, the program it is running, or the data you have created. ("Go ahead and try it—it won't snap at you.")

My techie friends assure me that such a scheme is outlandishly expensive and that only the biggest companies could mount such an effort. Maybe so. But I can imagine a multimedia training industry creating connect-the-dot formats that can quickly link data chunks on a disk to meet the requirements of individual users. The refusal to consider the idea only proves the original point—that technology companies are unwilling to meet users on users' terms.

> "For any system to adapt its external environment, its internal controls must incorporate variety. If one reduces variety inside the system, the system is unable to cope with variety in its external environment."
>
> *The Cybernetic Law of Requisite Variety*[7]

If they can't do this, what can they do instead to address the issue of user individuality?

WHAT YOU CAN DO TODAY

Let industry drag its feet. You can close the gap between them and yourself, by yourself.

If you are serious about lessening your techno craziness, you can't expect the industry to solve your problems. The burden of survival is always upon whoever wants to survive—hopefully, you.

Therefore it is up to each of us to look into our own nature and identify what our strengths and weaknesses as users are. And once we figure that out, to plot a path that will help us sidestep our natural shortcomings.

If you have a clear sense of your strong and weak suits, you can alert yourself to your own special brand of pitfalls. Here is a quickie questionnaire that pinpoints your dominant attitudes about technology. It won't tell you what kind of person you are—just what kind of computer person.

What Kind of Computer Person Are You?

Answer all questions with any number from 1 to 10.
Strongly agree = 10
Strongly disagree = 1
No strong feeling one way or the other = 5

A

1. _____ Technology is my friend. If I apply myself to mastering it, it will reward me accordingly.

2. _____ Technology is not for everyone. If you aren't willing to read the manual, you shouldn't use the application.

3. _____ I enjoy learning new programs and hearing about new technologies.

4. _____ People expect me to know my way around technology, and I don't want to let them down.

B

1. _____ Technology can be difficult, but people willing to apply themselves can usually master it.

2. _____ If I am given an assignment that requires that I learn to use a new program or how to use a machine, I usually succeed.

3. _____ I don't mind putting in a few hours of overtime to learn something.

4. _____ The workplace is a competition, and diligence in learning technology is a competitive advantage.

C

1. _____ There is nothing a computer can do that people working together cooperatively can't do equally well or even better.

2. _____ Given the choice between going to lunch with a friend or spending the time working on a database, I'll choose the friend nine times out of ten.

3. _____ People who are really good at technology often seem a little one-dimensional to me.

4. _____ My favorite office technology is the telephone.

D

1. _____ I can only do a few things using my PC, but I do them satisfactorily.

2. _____ You have to be able to master a few computer basics to hold down a job today.

3. _____ I sometimes have somebody else set up my system for me, but then I'm off and running.

4. _____ I'm not interested in how a machine works; I just want it to let me do my job.

E

1. _____ Computers are great, but I get myself into the strangest situations on them sometimes.

2. _____ I am an impulsive buyer. I sometimes buy programs or even whole systems that are not quite right for me.

3. _____ I get bored doing the same tasks day after day. I always like to be doing new things.

4. _____ When I take my system in to be fixed, it seems I am always assigned to the new guy.

F

1. _____ Each time I start my system up, I have a fantasy flash that it's broken.

2. _____ I feel embarrassed asking for help on my PC.

3. _____ I back my data up every day—sometimes even more often.

4. _____ I have plenty of protective devices in place—surge suppresser, power backup, dust cover, etc.

G

1. _____ People think I am really clever at times, doing my own thing on the computer. I even surprise myself.

2. _____ Technology is terrific. It may be our best chance at living better lives in the future.

3. _____ I don't like doing things the way the books say. I like to blaze my own trail.

4. _____ I see computer technology as a powerful tool for self-expression.

H

1. _____ Technology and I have never seemed able to get along together.

2. _____ When I learn a new program, I expect to learn it easily and without a lot of clumsy fumbling.

3. _____ I have been known to get angry at my PC.

4. _____ I'll be better at technology when technology gets better at meeting my needs.

I

1. _____ Computer technology leaves me cold. I don't like it, and I resent having to learn it.

2. _____ When I meet someone I'm told is talented at computers, I expect to dislike them a bit.

3. _____ What is the point of trying to catch up with technology at this stage of my life? I'll never catch up.

4. _____ I think computers turn people into numbers and make the world a duller place.

OK, now add up your scores. Add all the points under the A section and place it on the A line below; do the same with sections B through I.

A	POWER USER	_____
B	EARNEST LEARNER	_____
C	PEOPLE PERSON	_____
D	PLUGGER	_____
E	QUESTER	_____
F	WORRIER	_____
G	DREAMER	_____
H	SKEPTIC	_____
I	TECHNOPHOBE	_____

The type with the highest score is your dominant computing style. The low ranges describe your phantom, underdeveloped style. The midrange is mush. Most people who take this test end up with a scattered score: two or three types in the high range (from 31 to 40 points), two or three more in the middle range (11–30), and the rest in the low range (0–10).

While there is no right or wrong scoring, the preferred pattern is a broadly scattered one. A weird profile would show no scores in the middle range—this would likely be a very intense person, who careens from extreme to extreme.

Your challenge, should you accept this assignment, is to be more aware of your high and low ends—to keep the high end traits from eclipsing the other traits and to work at developing the phantom traits so that they, too, can be part of your arsenal.

Here are some keys to what your limitations are, and how to compensate for them:

- The **quester** faces an uphill struggle. You must first master yourself, then deal with technology. A machine is like a slab of Formica. It does not change from day to day. It is boring company for a chameleon personality—one that wakes up and has to reinvent itself every morning. Your best shot may be to motivate yourself to learn systems by doing things on them that you enjoy. Start surfing the World Wide Web on the Internet and visiting with newsgroups in the Usenet area that appeal to you—alt.unbalanced. loners, say, or rec.shaman.toad_lickers. We resist technology when it's no fun, or there's no enjoyment at the end of the struggle. Put a pot of gold at the end, and even you will beat a path to it.
- You are a **people person**, so you are skilled at identifying your lack of affinity with technology, and you realize it has much more to do with your social, organic personality than it has to do with the soul of the machine. You can forgive yourself for being born in the wrong century, and you make an extra effort to get with the program. Maybe you can focus on how your PC, the Internet, phones, and fax extend your ability to be social. Or maybe you can harness your natural power of persuasion to let a more systematic friend show you the ropes. Reading from a textbook won't work with you—you must be told and shown, in person.

- The **worrier's** problem is lack of confidence. You need to be shored up against your fears that the system you're working on is going to melt into a putty-colored puddle. If it helps you to take elaborate notes to perform chores, go for it. But what you really need is to be disabused, once and for all, of the idea that you present a clear and present danger to the system in front of you. Go to alt.folklore. computers in Usenet (or have someone do this for you) and ask the techno geeks that assemble there what they do to computers that annoy them. (They drop them from fourth-story windows, shoot them with guns, squirt lighter fluid on them and set them ablaze in parking lots.) Hardware is remarkably hard to kill, no matter how much you may want to. Walk out on the limb a little; you'll find it is sturdy enough for even you.

- As a **skeptic** you have preconceived feelings of negativity that prevent you from committing to a program or system. You fit the adage "once burned, twice shy." You are determined never to be made a fool of by some stupid computer again. But you are only holding yourself back. You need to forgive technology for always being in a state of flux, and yourself for stumbling and falling down the stairs a few times. A positive attitude toward technology begins with a streak of humility. That means setting aside your victim mentality and getting right back on the horse that just threw you.

- The **technophobe** has, as expected, the worst prospects. True technophobes are usually very interesting people, brimming with

SOFTWARE USERS' BILL OF RIGHTS

Users put up with a lot from the software industry. Now they are demanding a few basic considerations:

- The right to a standardized interface.
- The right to on-line help for every function.
- The right to learning without training.
- The right to expect mouse support for every program.
- The right to easy, thorough data import and export.
- The right to effective use of memory without crashing.
- The right to free support for 30 days.
- The right to same-day support callbacks.
- The right to systems and programs pre-optimized for top performance.[8]

values that you perceive to be under attack. Unfortunately, you bring all the wrong attributes to the technology table. For you to make peace with the millennium requires something approaching a complete makeover, and that kind of transformation is very seldom successful. The place to begin may be with the things the phobic user treasures: your sense of craft and your appreciation for excellence and individual differences. These are the same values, with a slight hitch in them, that drives software development teams and hardware engineers to create remarkable things. Somehow you must transfer or share allegiances. You must not feel you are betraying one world to peacefully co-exist with another. Finally, you must find the interface that is least off-putting, the one that most easily transports you out of "computing" and into the realm of work or play that you do not object to: being a journalist or a scholar or a correspondent or a business person. In short, you must buy a Mac.

Even types not currently queuing up on the ledge to jump because their computer is out to get them can benefit from this kind of self-assessment. Consider the four remaining types that fare reasonably well in the current system:

■ As a **dreamer** you get excited about new gadgets and then are disappointed when they don't work, or don't meet your expectations, or aren't as neat to work with as you imagined. First of all you need to get a handle on your expectations. No more late night computer magazine browsing, when the mind is weak

---

"MOST-WANTED"

HACKER NABBED

(Raleigh, NC.) After a search of more than two years, a team of FBI agents captured Kevin D. Mitnick, one of the most wanted computer criminals, accused of a crime spree that includes the theft of thousands of data files and at least 20,000 credit card numbers from computer systems around the nation.

On the run from federal law enforcement officials since November 1992, Mitnick used his sophisticated skills over the years to worm his way into the nation's telephone and cellular telephone networks and vandalize government, corporate, and university computer systems. Mitnick, already wanted in California for federal parole violations, was charged with federal crimes punishable by 20 years in prison and $500,000 in fines.[9]

and prone to strange cravings. People like you often see technology as the end in itself, not a means to an end. You buy things you have no practical use for—page scanners, backup power supplies, enormous database packages for teeny-weeny business applications. You need to find practical applications, things to do with your technology, work you can apply your dreaming to—instead of the technology itself.

> "The reduction of ambiguity to achieve certainty is the death of learning."
>
> *Linda Gloya*[10]

- The **plugger** is not quite the earnest user, but you stick with technologies until you are no longer a disgrace. You need to increase your comfort level with machines. Because you have no particular hang-ups about technology—you don't hate it, nor is your brain wired wrong for it—you are an excellent candidate for outside training. In the end your challenge is less with technology than with excellence itself. You must find what motivates you to do something well, and then get going.

- Our **earnest user** has a mild predicament. You are good at technology, and technology has made a terrific task-performer out of you. But it has also helped make you dull. All you want is to do your job, to meet specifications. You have better things to do in life besides make friends with your PC. You know you are competent, but you don't feel very special. You know your work is "good enough." But you also sense that "good enough" may not be good enough any more. Tomorrow's workers are going to be asked to routinely exceed specifications. Cogs need not apply. The recommendation here for earnest user is to get going. Start jogging. Get an easel and start daubing. Start developing that wild firebird spirit that is buried deep inside you somewhere.

- Finally, the **techno natural** or power user. We tend to think of you as the winner in the technology personality sweepstakes, and this whole technological century is your oyster, to crack and slurp down at your pleasure. On the contrary, you are in some ways as much a victim of technology as your opposite, the technophobe, because technology is often your master, and not the other way around. Seldom are you rewarded for your technological skills the way other people are for their financial or people skills. You are the sort who easily topples into obsessiveness, the fellow who stays up too late at his computer. Your insistence on being all-knowing in matters involving computers and systems borders on an unhealthy mania and is keeping you from doing your real work. People who truly love technology are most vulnerable to its power—to distract, to confuse. People like you need to restore balance to your lives—before you have none at all.

Remember that the "highest" type represented here, the techno natural, though he is great with technology, does not run the world.[11]

Most technos feel that their love of technology is actually a strike against them. Very few corporate leaders come up through their ranks. For heaven's sakes, they call themselves nerds. They have a facility for machines, but they suffer, too, in different ways from the rest of us. They get hit not on the downside, by avoidance and fear, but on the topside, by mania and imbalance. Think of all the techno wizards that lose their jobs every time a new technology obsoletes an old one, or when the stock market hiccups. Think of all the families that never see Dad because he is sitting at a console all weekend, or Mom because she is up late solving some riddle in C++. There are as many computer widows as football widows, and the number of computer widowers is on the rise.

> "A human being should be able to change a diaper, plan an invasion, butcher a hog, conn a ship, design a building, write a sonnet, balance accounts, build a wall, set a bone, comfort the dying, take orders, give orders, cooperate, act alone, solve equations, analyze a new problem, pitch manure, program a computer, cook a tasty meal, fight efficiently, die gallantly. Specialization is for insects."
>
> *Robert Heinlein*[12]

Some techno naturals are so intense that it wrecks their lives. They venture just a bit too far into the darker realms of cyberspace. Think of virus-maker Robert Tappan Morris, son of a world-famous computer security expert, who created and unleashed the Internet Worm upon the ARPAnet network, shutting down much of this country's defense intelligence systems overnight. Brilliant, ingenious, and by all accounts idealistic, Robert Morris is still on probation, done in by the thing he most loved.

MAKE UP YOUR MIND

If you can't abide all this talk about personality, you must still reckon with the universal plight of users today. People trying to make sense of a very difficult realm have three choices:

1. They can say thanks but no thanks to technology and walk away from the modern world.

2. They can cry themselves to sleep every night and hope things are better the next day. Maybe they will. Remember, "Microsoft cares."

3. They can stop being afraid of what might happen and start taking responsibility for what they want to accomplish.

Bypassing fear lies at the very heart of techno wisdom. It is not easy because fear is never superficial. It occurs deeper in you than the conscious thoughts you can marshal against it. Your task is to disarm the fear, not "overcome" it via courage or stoicism or brute will power. The way to disarm fear is with countervailing experience.

Here are some oblique strategies for short-circuiting your fear impulses:

- **Fight your type.** If you are a true technophobe, find some dimension of technology to get behind. Maybe it is the history of technology, biographies of computer scientists, Internet discussion rooms (newsgroups) that are fun for you. Sneak by the thing about technology that you don't like by embracing things that you do like. This puts you in the game and learning; half the battle, right there.
- **Relax.** Realize that no one is comfortable with the whole of technology, not even the techies who make cracks at your fumble-fingeredness. No one has a comprehensive grasp of all the different hardware and software platforms. They are technophobic, too, just in a lesser degree than you. They act comfortable in front of you, but that's because they know you can't challenge them. They are cyber bullies, covering up their own insecurities.

We all have dreams about technology. For some of us the dream is smooth sailing. Clean and progressive and engaging and alive, every day a new surprise and a pleasure. For others of us it's a nightmare, with machines demanding more from us, faster than we can keep up.

49

The very strong temptation is to place the blame and responsibility for making it better on the shoulders of the industry. They caused the problem; let them fix it.

But they will never fix the problem. It is technology's business to be new, and being new—really new—will always cause a gap between product and public comprehension, no matter how the product bulletproofs itself with training manuals, CD-ROMs, etc.

If all else fails, pack it in for a while, get out of the house, and step out into the real world, where the only digital things are your fingers, and even they have stopped drumming.

CHAPTER ■

Communicating with Computer People

What to Look for, What to Ask for, and How to Say It

In which the techno neophyte must do verbal battle with tech support, direct mail order takers, colleagues, electronic correspondents, and the English language

Technology thrusts a host of new social circumstances upon us—circumstances that take most of us wholly by surprise. Forget the truly intense communication arenas—how we incorporate computing into our dealings with friends, family, neighbors, and colleagues. You can successfully miscommunicate about computing even with people who are fluent in computerese. This chapter covers the gamut of these communication bottlenecks, from purchasing snafus to rotten e-mail manners.

When we first decided to buy a computer, for instance, we never imagined it would be difficult dealing with sales clerks or mail house operators. When we went on-line, all gung-ho to connect with a thousand points around the world, we had no manual for how to talk to people. Heck, we never thought it would be a challenge just describing our system to our neighbor over the backyard fence.

But all these circumstances do call for special responses and considerations. Here are some hints on how to negotiate the social shoals of technology.

DEALING WITH CUSTOMER SERVICE AND TECH SUPPORT

Wouldn't it be great if every time you bought a new piece of software or a hardware add-on, it installed itself without a hassle? I think that when people live really good lives, and then they die, and they go to heaven, that is what happens. There are no dip switches to set in heaven.

Meanwhile, we are stuck in this vale of tears, ESCape codes, and IRQ interrupts. Problems happen and users need help. But how good is the customer service that is available today? How has it changed from customer service in years gone by? And how can users best avail themselves of the expertise that is out there for them?

Customer assistance varies widely from company to company and from type of company to type of company. Most low-end direct market outfits make no bones about the fact that their priority is keeping prices low. When installation instructions show not even a hint of an understanding of the English language ("The Baby I/O, it can be used by all personal Computers which are compatible with 16 Bit Personal Computer") [1], it's a fair bet that their tech support is no better.

> "The computer is down. I hope it's something serious."
>
> *Stanton Delaplane* [2]

Likewise, the farther the product seller is from the product developer, the less likely the seller is to have solid first-hand knowledge of the product. Though there are exceptions, retailers, resellers, and other third parties usually do not know how to run what they sell.

The best source of technical support is usually the manufacturer. Some have been very good indeed. WordPerfect Corp., considered for many years to be the top customer-support company in the industry, was almost alone for over a decade in offering unlimited free 1-800 customer service during working hours. Indeed, WordPerfect provided a half dozen 800 numbers you could call, one each for installation, features, graphics/macros, laser printers, dot-matrix printers, and other printers and networks.

Think about that for a moment. You could buy WordPerfect for about $200 anywhere. Of that, a third went to the retailer. That left less than $140 for the WordPerfect Corporation. Now let's say the average customer used the customer support number six times in the four-year course of owning the program, for 20 minutes each time.

Two hours is not much time spread over four years. But it was plenty expensive for WordPerfect Corp., easily a $100 value, considering the cost of training customer support people and paying them, plus the overhead of maintaining phone banks. That left about $40 to pay WordPerfect's noncustomer support costs—development, manufacturing, and advertising. It was a bargain not every customer appreciated.

It meant that a third of all WordPerfect employees did customer service. Compare that to one tenth of all Microsoft's employees. WordPerfect wrote it off as a marketing expense, and it was true that Microsoft spends a lot more by percentage on conventional marketing. For its trouble WordPerfect could claim a much higher level of customer retention; such extensive customer support is a competitive advantage.

And now the other shoe drops. When WordPerfect Corp. merged with Novell in 1994, it pared its support to levels comparable to the rest of the industry. No more unlimited 800 calls. The proportion of support to nonsupport staff is returning to industry norms.

It's tempting to criticize companies that nickel-and-dime their customers. Where do they get off charging us to tell us how their products work? Imagine if Chrysler did that, or MCI? Where would they get their next customers? One wants to sigh, but what good would it do.

There are three most-used in-between tech support measures:

> "The most overlooked advantage to owning a computer is that if they foul up there's no law against whacking them around a little."
>
> *Stan Porterfield*[3]

- A company can meet you halfway with pay-toll technical support, in which you pay for the long-distance charge but not the support itself. A hybrid is to offer free support for the first 90 days after you buy the product, after which time you pay for the call.
- A company can protect itself to the maximum by making you pay for both the call and for the support, on an extended warranty or fee basis. Companies defend this practice by saying that it puts the cost for support where it belongs—on the shoulders of people who have a hard time figuring things out and not on the average customer, thus holding down product price.

1617. John Napier, the wealthy Baron of Merchiston, outside Edinburgh, Scotland, is a hobbyist mathematician. He is famous today among math types for inventing logarithms, numbers that simplify multiplication and division to addition and subtraction. He also invents a forerunner of the tank, an armed chariot containing several musketeers. He designs mirrors that can set fire to faraway ships, perhaps making him the intellectual godfather of Star Wars. But computer historians will remember him for devising a contraption of sliding rods called Napier's Bones, allowing struggling scientists of the modern era to make rapid logarithmic calculations.

(Continued on page 55)

■ A company can have a drop-in service center in your city. This is more a hardware phenomenon than a software one. Epson, IBM, Everex, Panasonic, and other companies do this. But beware—most service centers are profit centers. While they can answer questions for you, as soon as you push your system across the counter, the meter is running.

Most major brands also employ secondary technical support services, like newsletters, electronic bulletin board systems (BBSes), and user forums. Newsletters are too slow for expeditious problem-solving, but they are great at broadcasting general solutions to common problems.

BBSes are a good low-cost way to call with a problem in the morning and call back for the solution later that day. A variant is the tech support FAX line, where you send in your problem and they call you back. Most companies pick up the tab for the callback, but not all.

User forums, like the ones conducted on CompuServe and America Online, are a low-budget solution. While cheaper for the caller than a long-distance call, users must subscribe to the on-line service. And replies can sometimes be days in coming.

Now, none of these solutions will make you 100 percent happy. Even the WordPerfect solution causes gnashing of teeth when you absolutely, positively must finish a document by 3:00 p.m. and the phone lines to Utah are jammed with callers with less serious problems, blithely taking advantage of the free support.

Two bad things can happen when you call a tech support number. You can get an endless busy signal, which means you have to sit at your desk, sometimes for an hour or more, redialing the number. After a while you want to scream through the receiver for your vendor to hang up and answer the phone.

The other bad thing is that the phone will answer, and a machine will politely queue you up, at your expense, behind God-knows-how-many other waiting parties. For all you know, there is only one tech support rep handling the phones that day, and the line is 10,000 people long, and the person currently being served is a gentleman from Nashua, New Hampshire, wanting to know where he can get a printer driver for a teletype machine he bought at a rummage sale in Black River Junction for $10. Not knowing for sure, the mind plays vile tricks while the voicemail Muzak plays "I Am the Walrus" as performed by John Williams and the Boston Pops. Goo goo ka choob.

There are other problems with technical support. One is that you never know in advance what a company's policies are. If you go to Computer City to buy a presentation manager, how do you know whether Lotus's Freelance Graphics for Windows or Microsoft PowerPoint has the cheaper or more complete technical support? That information is buried deep down in the manuals. The clerk can assure you that the store will answer your questions, but they don't know anything. Even the oral promise of "free technical support" is riddled with loopholes.

1621. Rev. William Oughtred, an Englishman, follows up on Napier's investigations. Not unusual for scientists of that day, Oughtred is torn between his fascination with numbers and his love of God. His big contribution is fashioning the first slide rule, which he calls "Circles of Proportion." He is hailed as a genius, and he tutors some of the brightest up-and-coming mathematicians at Oxford.

1630. One of Oughtred's students is one Richard Delamain, who causes quite a stir claiming that he, not Oughtred, had invented the slide rule. Oughtred is outraged, and the two go at each other in print and in public for many years. This happens long before future intellectual property squabbles between Microsoft, Apple, Lotus, Adobe, and everyone else. Eventually they agree to split credit for the device, and Delamain goes on to become math tutor to Charles II, who had quite a head for numbers himself, for a time.

But if you are the sort of person who leans heavily on tech support services, you'd better do some preliminary homework, even if it means calling the companies in advance. Find out such things as the exact hours of toll-free phone support, and how long after your purchase tech support is free. Find out if the company has special arrangements for users who are support-intensive—an extended warranty or third-party arrangement.

If you are a volume buyer, strike a deal for your company. There's no reason why, if you have bought $2 million worth of Microsoft products this year, you should have to get in line behind Joe Schmoe for customer assistance. Oligopolies have rights, too!

Look for companies that offer specific service guarantees. Any time you see an unconditional guarantee in an ad—satisfaction guaranteed or your money back—that company has assumed the burden of getting you on track and happy again, and hang the expense. Such a guarantee may even cover repairs.

We are lucky to be living in a time when quality service is one way for otherwise plain-vanilla companies to distinguish themselves. Compaq and Dell have ridden the quality rails to glory. Let them take you for a ride, too.

What can you do to make the whole tech support experience work better? Here are some fine points of phone etiquette. Read them, and next time you are up a tree with a software or hardware problem, remember them before dialing your tech support rep.

- **Pull yourself together.** Sure, you're having a lousy day. That's nothing new to tech support reps—they converse almost solely with tormented souls just like yourself. Don't play the victim. A positive mental attitude adds years to your life span, unless you thrive on being a crab.
- **Have a clue.** Have important information handy. What version of the software you have, and what operating system you are running. Your serial number, if possible. Have your CONFIG.SYS and AUTOEXEC. BAT files printed out, for quick reference. (This is irrelevant if you are calling with a printer problem.)
- **Shake your floppy.** It often helps to have a bootable diskette ready. A booted disk is a floppy for your A: drive that you have formatted with the system files on it. By booting this diskette, you bypass your hard disk and all the complicated instructions there that may be causing your problems.

- **Don't play doctor.** Don't tell the tech service rep in advance what the diagnosis is. Let him or her have some of the fun. Describe the problem—what happens that keeps you from doing what you want to do. Let the tech service rep take it from there.
- **Write things down.** Get your tech rep's name, so the next time you call you aren't a voice out of the void. Sure, some companies overload you with requirements—return authorization numbers, etc. But, like they say, they do it "to serve you better."
- **Be nice.** It's so easy, in the stress you are feeling, to launch into a host of sideswipe attacks on anything and everything associated with the company in question—its inscrutable documentation, its endless call lines, its useless help files, and so forth. Realize that you are firing blanks—the rep has heard every blast you can make five times before lunch every day. He's rubber and you're glue—everything you say bounces off him and sticks to you.

Finally, do you want to hear a sad, terrible, unfortunate, obvious truth? Big companies generally provide better service. They are interested in retaining customers, not just snaring them for one-time purchases. Big companies can afford to keep an extra dozen tech support people sitting around waiting for the phone to ring. They can better absorb training costs and more easily attract talented people. They can also afford the switching and routing technology to make the most of those people.

> "When I am speaking to one party and a second party is calling, how do I decide which one to continue to speak to, and which one gets put on hold? One is forced to make an on-the-spot judgment that inevitably leads to all sorts of guilt feelings."
>
> *Marc Bryan-Brown*[4]

Small companies have a much harder time assimilating a sudden influx of calls. That is why it is sometimes better to buy a B+ product that is a standard from a Big 10 company than an A+ product from a start-up that has its hands full with its success.

I wish to heaven that were not true, and sometimes it isn't, but usually it is. The exceptions can be glorious—I am thinking of a tech support person at AddStor, the data compression utility company, who once gave me the better part of three hours of on-line help while I read

brain dump—Spilling all. Divulging everything. Core heave.

brain damage—See *Pentium*.

computer—In the old days, a person who sat on a tall stool, adding up figures. Nowadays, it refers to a machine performing the same function, run by a person in a regular chair.

divide by zero—MIT mathematician Norbert Wiener tried to test Siblitz's first electronic computer using Boolean as opposed to digital logic, at a remarkable presentation in 1938, at which Wiener tried to trick the computer into dividing by zero—something undoable, a schoolboy's trick. Divide by zero has been the programmer's nemesis ever since—it is the standard error message for millions of program bugs. A black hole has been described as God's attempt to divide by zero.

him verbatim my CONFIG.SYS, AUTOEXEC.BAT, WIN.INI and SYSTEM.INI files, character by character. Somewhere in line 114 he found the offending parameter, fixed it, and I drew breath again.

After he fixed me up, I realized I never caught his name.

COMMUNICATING WITH MAIL HOUSES

When I bought my first computer in 1983, buying by mail order was unthinkable. Computers were so finicky, and the mood of the public so dubious, that customers needed to duplicate the secure, kick-the-tires flavor of an automobile showroom.

Within a few years, the invasion of the clones struck, and it was no longer so important to pick the right brand of computer—they were all very nearly the same computer. In a clone market, the need to kick tires dwindled, and the purchase decision was based much more on price. Some of the best bargains were sold directly from the mail house (Dell, Northgate, Gateway, Zeos) to you.

The ad campaigns radiated confidence. The mail order clones (phone order clones, really) were not only just as good as actual IBMs and Compaqs (this was before these two started their own discount direct sales outposts), they were in some ways better.

Their prices were lower, of course. But price was just the beginning. Ordering without leaving home and delivery to your door means convenience. Customer service numbers and tech support guarantees are better support commitment than some stores offer. If you buy out-of-state you often avoid state sales taxes, which can amount to hundreds on a system sale.

The technological evolution caused people to evolve as well. We were suddenly charged with the bravery to buy the most complicated, most fragile thing we would ever buy, from people we would never see, to be trucked to us by people who scarcely cared. Computing was finally and fully the great adventure of our lives. Today, a third of all systems are bought this way.

But you have to know how to do it. It may not, for instance, be the best way to buy a single system. Large companies love buying 500 PCs at a shot from Gateway or Dell, because they know they are getting 500 identical boxes, with identical chips, processors, cards, etc. Big-company information services departments have a much easier time fixing and modifying identical PCs than those with a zillion different nonstandard components. You, buying a mail-order computer from out of town, may end up with a system just different enough to your local repair team that they will have trouble fixing it.

> "Is this the party to whom I am speaking?"
>
> *Lily Tomlin, as Ernestine*[5]

That happened to me once. I brought my clone in to be repaired. The repairman really took a shine to my machine. He said it was "ingeniously put together." It fit two IDE type hard drives in a very compact space, leaving room for a mess of other drives. It had more expansion space than a circus tent.

For a moment I was pretty proud of myself for stumbling upon vendors through the mail who really knew their engineering. But the repairman quickly dashed that pride. "Yeah, I think you should pack this up and truck it back to them for repairs."

Which I did. Dragged my original cardboard and styrofoam down from the garage eaves, packed the computer carefully, wrapped it and taped it, labeled it for UPS, and called the Maryland company I had bought it from to get a return authorization number.

"I'm sorry," a faraway voice said, "the number you have dialed is no longer in service."

Eventually I found a local repair person who could fix my problem, but I never did find my computer company again.

You have to be super careful to ask the right questions when dealing with mail order people. A previous mail order experience had been a disaster. The trucking company shipping my brand new

THE ETIQUETTE OF POKING AROUND IN SOMEONE ELSE'S SYSTEM

A few helpful do's and don'ts to observe in the delicate business of poking around inside other people's equipment:

- **First, get all spouses out of the room.** All day long he or she has been giving your friend hell for spending the furnace money on a computer in the first place. (That's probably your fault, too.) Spouses are "bad cops." If they hang around, arms crossed, toes tapping on the shag rug, your resolve will weaken like nobody's business.

- **Never show fear.** If you waffle at the prospect of cracking open a tape drive with a screwdriver, or tapping it with a ball peen hammer, or poking it with a barbecue fork, what good are you to your friend in need? You wouldn't want to wake up in the middle of open heart surgery and see your doctor holding your heart in his hand with an insecure expression up above the surgical mask, where his eyebrows are, would you?

(Continued on page 61)

Hewlett-Packard LaserJet III from Boston to Minnesota somehow let it fall off the back of the truck just south of Toledo, subdividing the printer into eleven pieces.

When I decided to buy a PC for my brother in San Francisco I didn't want that to happen again, so I called a mail order shop located right in the Bay Area. I specifically asked about delivery. How long would it take? Oh, about four days. Do you have a good shipper? Yes, tip-top, A-OK.

I bought the PC, waited four days, and called my brother. No, it hadn't arrived yet. After seven days, no, not yet. When it hadn't arrived ten days later, I called the company, located 65 miles from my brother's front door, and was told it wouldn't arrive for another week. Why? Because it took that long to ship from their warehouse in New Jersey.

"But, but" I sputtered, "your ad shows you are in San Mateo."

"Phones are here. Warehouse is in Newark."

I pictured the computer bouncing around on a flat-bed truck, finally tumbling off into a sun-baked cowcake somewhere around Cheyenne. Sure enough, the thing finally arrived in San Francisco with a very minor problem—a drive cable had come loose. But I couldn't diagnose it from my place in Minnesota, and my poor brother—a classic, certifiable technophobe—had no way of knowing what the "BOOT FAIL-URE" message meant, and even if he had known he wouldn't have known how to unscrew the back of the box and reconnect the cables.

Mail order poses difficulties of the simplest sort. One's sense of time and space are easily disoriented. You can't see the face of the person you're giving thousands of your dollars to—he could have long curly horns and carry a trident with him to work every day. For all you know, he could be a disembodied brain in a petrie dish, with voice synthesizer and a bad baking soda habit. Face-to-face, these things are tip-offs; on the phone, they're nothing.

In a way, the mail order situation typifies all the problems of computing generally. If you are buying a first system, it is a foreshadowing of what is to come—impersonal treatment, ambiguous communications, and trying to do something across a vast unknowable region of imaginary space. You might consider mail order as a test of your computing future. If you can buy a computer by mail success-fully—getting what you want, the way you want it, for the price you wanted to pay—you are going to be a star at the console.

Here are some of the things most often miscommunicated:

- Your operating system. DOS, Windows, Warp OS/2, UNIX, Mac System 7.5, etc.

- **Don't ask permission—ask forgiveness.** The moment friends ask your advice, they empower you to do what you think best. No hand-holding, no charts and graphs, no bib-liography, and no cost-benefit analysis. Just dive in there and start yanking.

- **Put humor in your toolkit.** Keep up a lively patter while disassembling. Let your friend be in charge of the things you pull out, like the little screws. When it's time to put them back in, tell him it's very vital that he hand them back to you in the order you gave them to him. The look on his face is worth the price of admission.

- **Accentuate the positive.** You wouldn't be knee-deep in your friend's transistors if some-thing wasn't wrong some-where. Chances are something will need replacing, and some of these things cost money. If you squeeze a little hard on the chip extractor, and the chip caves in, quickly allay your friend's needless worry. These computer parts aren't designed to last forever, after all. Tip: Think of peripherals as fan belts; early and frequent re-placement is the surest way to guarantee a long and purpose-ful life for your computer.

(Continued on page 62)

■ **When you screw up, make like it's a breakthrough in human knowledge.** No one expects perfection, just a good honest effort. When you fall measurably short of perfection, take solace in lessons learned. I can't begin to convey how comforting it has been to hear me say things like, "You know, the manufacturer of these diskettes should put warnings on the sleeves about the dangers of microwave ovens," or "PC Magazine pays $50 and a T-shirt for stories like this one about what happens when you hook up a laptop to a car battery."

■ **Expect no reward for all your kindnesses.** How typical it is of human nature: you come to your friends' assistance, you open their computers, and in the course of your examination you accidentally tip a beaker of boysenberry pancake syrup over the keyboard. Hey, it happens. But do your friends rush in, as real friends are supposed to, to reassure you that it's all right? No, they turn on you like vicious rabid dogs.

(Continued on page 63)

■ How your peripheral is to be connected. Whether serial or parallel, whether to an old ISA bus or the newer VL bus, or conforming to new Plug and Play requirements. Whether a mouse uses a regular PC driver or a nonstandard one like PS/2.

■ Who pays for shipping. Whether the out-of-state store still charges you that state's sales tax. Who pays return shipping in case of problems. How long shipping will take (overnight air or overdue camel).

■ Is there a charge for using a credit card? This is especially obnoxious in a business that only accepts credit cards.

■ Whether the new machine will accept your old machine's peripherals without new cards or cables.

■ What is included and what is not (monitor, modem, CD-ROM, video card, soundcard, mouse, software, etc.)

■ What will be preinstalled and what you will have to do yourself.

These are points you fully intended to ask on the phone, but in the heat of the moment, and the preciousness of daytime long-distance calling, you didn't.

You need to know, if you are buying on the cheap side, if you are mistakenly ordering one of last year's laptops, not this year's. (Last year's laptops always stink, this year's are always the breakthrough models. This is true regardless of the actual year.)

When buying from direct mail liquidation outlets, sight unseen, weird things can happen. Years ago, a friend opened a shipping crate and found, not a generic, putty-colored box, but a shiny-plastic, lemon-yellow box with border-decals of daffodils and anemones surrounding a plate that read "LADY DATA." At least at a physical liquidation outlet you get to see the horrific marketing errors before you bail them out.

My experience has been that it's much more pleasant buying from an established mail order factory like Gateway or Dell than from a mail order catalog offering a wide range of products. People who only sell systems need less training than people who sell systems plus software plus computer furniture, and they will be able to help you more. Systems sales people have a program running which configures your dream system for you, telling you exactly how much more, for instance, a PCMCIA slot will add to your total. And they will let you know if your request is out of kilter—your hard drive is too small or your power supply too big. Direct marketing superstores sell on price, period—they won't be able to help you choose between WordPerfect or Microsoft Word.

What are the chances you will get completely shafted—that a company will take your money and not send you what you ordered? About one in a hundred. The problem isn't outright fraud so much as companies playing the Chapter Eleven game, in which they take money from new orders and use it to pay outstanding bills—so you become the new outstanding bill, bye bye and good luck.

You are especially vulnerable to this ploy if you order by check—another reason to always use a credit card, because the card issuer has a relationship with the retailer and will intercede on your behalf. If you demand a chargeback from your card company, in writing and separate from your monthly bill payment, they are obliged by law to at least think about it.

■ **Start deflecting blame early.** Ideally, before the first plume of smoke appears. Say things like, "Man, don't you ever vacuum in here?" Or, "Looks like a classic case of penny-wise and dollar foolish." Or, "Are you sure you read the installation manual from cover to cover before booting up?" Take a tip from the major players: It's always the end-user's fault.

DON'T BE A NEWBIE

Every month thousands of new subscribers swarm into the Usenet newsrooms of the Internet. Most are nonplused at the cold welcome they receive.

Usenet newcomers, or *newbies*, are held in the lowest regard by Internet veterans. The phrase newbie originated in British public schools and is short for "new boy." It first surfaced on the net in the talk.bizarre newsroom in 1993 and is now part of the parlance.

Newbies may be tolerated if they are sincere or appear educable. More often they are excoriated for being, as a class, stupid, illiterate, uncivil, underage, chromosomally clueless, and undoubtedly hailing from one of the odious meganodes (Delphi was the most reviled, until AOL users flooded the net, earning butthead bragging rights).

To avoid the opprobrium of being a newbie, eschew:

- **Posting a chain letter** or publishing fast-money solicitations.
- **Blathering,** going on and on pointlessly, or posting an "urban legend" as true. ("Well, a friend of a friend told me . . .")

(Continued on page 65)

You have other options, as well. First off, call the company. Don't go running to the Feds until you're satisfied you've been good and shafted. If the company rep stonewalls you, ask to talk to someone else. Put your problem in writing, and hold on to your copies—that goes for all receipts, bills of lading, ads you ordered from, etc.

If that fails, or if you bought with a personal check, then complain to your local postal inspector. I know, that sounds like throwing the family dog down the well, but it sometimes works. The postal service has a fair reputation for enforcing mail regulations, in contrast to the Federal Trade Commission, which has oodles of mail fraud regulations in print but is said to be indifferent to individual claims.

And if neither of these agencies can help, contact the Mail Order Action Line of the mail order industry's professional association, the Direct Marketing Association (6 East 43rd Street, New York NY 10017). They are hot to root out firms that make the profession look bad, and they will offer to act as a liaison to resolve your dispute.

I-Ways and Byways

You walk through a bookstore these days and immediately stand in the shadow of an enormous stack of Internet navigators, explorers, and voyagers, under a galleon of different imprints, that, if it toppled and fell on you, would beat you into creamed corn.

People are swarming onto the Internet in unprecedented numbers, in a vast virtual migration. The net is said to be growing by about 20 percent every month. One company after another is leapfrogging its way into the cyber regions, though no one has made any real money there yet. Total sales made on the Internet in 1994, for instance, were a negligible $200 million—less than $3 per user.[6]

The big commercial on-line services are playing a big role in the rush. Single-handedly, America Online and Delphi have mongrelized the Usenet newsgroups. Prodigy is next, with plans to dump its teeming masses upon the unsuspecting World Wide Web. God only knows how choked the info thoroughfare will be now that CompuServe is equipping its 2 million users on full-scale Internet surfboards.

To make things worse, the really big boys have been weighing in this past month. Microsoft is building Internet dial-up capabilities into Windows 95, with World Wide Web, the graphic Internet network (that is what people talk about when talking about "surfing the net") available as an option. AT&T and MCI are likewise entertaining impe-

- **Crossposting** (spewing) the following familiar message to all 7000 newsgroups: "Anyone there? Please rite as I luv to get mail."
- **Including the entire text** of the message you are responding to, or worse, including no contextual clues whatsoever.
- **Unwisely adding a 12-line signature** file at the end of every message, that comes out doubled with every post.
- **Never using upper case.** OR MUCH, MUCH WORSE, NEVER USING LOWER CASE. It's . . . screamy.
- **Posting antediluvian copier room humor** (i.e., "Murphy's Laws"). What was funny once is fossilized now.
- **Posting in B1FF-speak** ("B1FF IZ A Kk001 d0oD!!@ !!")
- **Responding to "flamebait"** everyone else is weary of. Net vets do not wish to discuss the divinity of Jesus, particularly in the **alt.cyberpunk** room. Since they're tired of it, they ask that you be, too.
- **Taking a flamer seriously** that no one else does. The ignorant newcomer overreacts to a net-troll everyone else pretends isn't there. It only encourages them.

(Continued on page 66)

And by all means do:

- **Be cool.** Don't post in a group until you've read it for a few weeks, and developed a feel for what kind of people hang out there.
- **Master netiquette.** Neither a flamebaiter nor a flamer, a blatherer nor a net-weenie be. There are books (like *The Elements of E-mail Style*, by David Angell and Brent Heslop, Addison-Wesley) to guide you through the e-mail minefield.
- **Read the FAQs** (Frequently Asked Question files). Most serious newsgroups have one. If you have FTP, you can download just about any FAQ from **rtfm.mit.edu.**
- **Use newlines.** Break the lines of your posts before they exceed 80 characters.
- **When in doubt, lurk.** Be inconspicuous until you get the lay of the land.
- **Hie thee** to the newsgroup **news.announce.newusers** and read all the basic articles about using UseNet that show up in there, for about a month (until they start to repeat). There's about 12 or 15 of them.

(Continued on page 67)

rial ambitions regarding cyberspace. They are planning Internet access programs of their own. That news surely sends a shiver down the vertebra of every mom and pop gateway operator this side of Little America.

Amidst this climate of craziness, it might be wise to consider some of the serious shortcomings to traveling the I-Ways in our time:

- **What superhighway?** The superhighway everyone talks about so ecstatically—everything hooked up to everything, superfast transmission, transparent user interfaces—does not exist yet. Internet software, though it improves by leaps and bounds every six months, is still hard to use and confusing. It is not as big (70 million users) as people are saying. A closer figure is 120 million regular users worldwide[7] in mid-1995—though it is doubling annually. The sheer volume of traffic brings everyone to a slow crawl—Monday morning being the worst.
- **The language is, like, Hittite.** Net users of the future will be astonished that we had to learn the difference between FTP, HTML, gopher, and Telnet. Entirely too many books about the UNIX command language have been written and sold.
- **People are rude.** The most unpleasant awakening of all is to

find out just how unfriendly people on the nets can be. There is a perpetual war between veterans and newbies, those who know and are in a position to dictate net etiquette, and those too new to the environment to fit in. At their worst the newbies are guests who overstep their welcome. At their worst, the veterans are officious funkillers—like teenaged lifeguards who let their whistles go to their heads.

■ **The network of networks is not networked.** By this I mean, while commercial on-line services are unilaterally providing access to much of the Internet for their customers, the freedom of access is not reciprocal. A CompuServe customer can't look around in America Online. An Internet gateway subscriber cannot examine the treasures of Prodigy.

■ **You never find what you are looking for.** Spend an afternoon grappling with the big on-line

■ **Take your time** by "marking" an article that interests you as "unread." If, after reading the entire thread, no one has made the point you wish to make, you may sally forth and make it yourself.

■ **Be of good cheer.** We all are newbies when we start—and remain so in all newsgroups till we familiarize ourselves with them all—which no one ever does.

Remember: these wizened veterans (some of them all of 17 years old) wouldn't be so cruel to the clueless if they weren't insecure about something themselves. Chances are good that the person slamming you is only a little less moist behind the cyber ears.

research databases and you will know the meaning of research pain. The guiding vision behind these databases (Knowledge Index, Orbit, Dialog, IQuest, Magazine DataBase Plus, Lexis, etc.) is to compile abstracts and full-text versions of every article ever published, along with every item in every major reference title (*Who's Who, Books in Print*, etc.). But to find them you must craft search strings using the hit-or-miss language of Boolean symbolic logic. Too often, the article you need simply can't be located this way, or you can't think of the right search strings to look for. Mistakes cost money. A lot of mistakes lead one to quit looking altogether.

■ **Data is overpriced.** If you want to find a magazine article on the net, expect either not to find it or to pay a premium price when you do find it. The Internet itself offers some data sources, but they are random and incomplete. Commercial databases like Lexis and Dialog are outlandishly expensive, costing thousands per year. This is a real controversy. Should nonproprietary information be the captive of commercial interests? That is what Lexis thinks: they deserve $7 per citation because they take such good care of it. Or should it be free? That is the prejudice of Internet old-timers—but their information is spotty and often outdated. Ideally, we will end up somewhere in the middle, paying enough to reward the added value of maintenance but not paying an arm and a leg for something that costs the vendor nothing.

■ **It is a security sieve.** Despite all the talk of big business taking over the net, it has been a very slow rush. More of an ooze, really. The reason—corporations are reluctant to enter into an interactive data relationship with everyone in the world. Hackers, phreakers, and late-night mischief makers adore finding chinks in digital firewalls and seeing what is inside. Do you want to post your Visa number on an insecure network? One of the many ironies of the net is that it was founded as a reliable national security platform for government/ military communications in the 1960s, and today it is so huge and so diverse and so unreliable that the government and military would be crazy to use it for anything even halfway confidential.

■ **It is anarchic.** The Internet itself is a tremendously free-wheeling place, where freedom of speech is the paramount value—often to the exclusion of the simple decencies we prize in our non-net lives. Before one can locate the alt.bible.study.cookies newsgroup, one may first have to walk a gauntlet of purveyors of kiddie porn; freaked-out, armed-to-the-teeth conspiracy buffs; starry-eyed, get-rich-quick schemers; teenagers just discovering the rhetorical impact of four-letter words; and sad, sick psychotics who stalk and terrorize their e-prey. This is not to everyone's taste. Worse, it is the pandering politician's dream issue. Yet how do you clamp down on the hideous and the odd without impinging the rights of all? Indeed, in a decentralized network, how could an aroused government achieve centralized controls a la *1984*?

■ **It is not anarchic enough.** Different parts of the I-Way play by different rules, and it is the responsibility of the visitor to learn and live by them. A new class of room moderators, system operators and administrators, traffic cops, list managers, and anchor users has arisen to act as judges of what is acceptable and what is unacceptable. Many newsgroups have their own detailed rules of engagement (FAQ or Frequently Asked Questions files) that one must study. These people can be very annoying, as when they inform you that a post that took you 25 minutes to compose, and posted to a room full of people you are dying to address, has been obliterated because it violated Question #114 on that newsgroup's FAQ.

■ **Too much, too soon.** The worst thing about living on the net is that things are changing so rapidly that information molds over before it is published. Why do Internet books waste 80 pages listing Usenet newsgroups when a third of all entries will be empty shells by the time a reader tries to visit them, and another, unlisted third will have sprung into existence? The World Wide Web is a great example. In 1993, there was no such thing. In 1994, one needed Mosaic software to access it. In 1995, no one was creating Web pages for Mosaic any more; NetScape had replaced it as the de facto standard. And so it goes, and will go, for the foreseeable future: net riders will have to step nimbly to avoid tripping on last year's information.

For all but techno naturals, there is only one cure for hard times on the I-Way, and that is to calculate exactly how much aggravation you are willing to put up with, and stick to that level. Researchers have always had alternative options to on-line research, and they can stick to those until on-line searches become easier to do. (Warning: most library catalog systems now also use Boolean search logic.)

Meanwhile, put down your heavy burden and wait. Better software is coming. The hypertext surfing style of the World Wide Web will end the necessity of knowing the difference between FTP, gopher, and Telnet. Somehow soon, a combination of new modems, new wires, new software and new structure will combine to create a faster, simplified, lower-cost system. It may be some consolation to the newbies of the net that, for all the grief they endure, it was they and not net veterans who forced the network of networks to finally adapt to human beings.

Etiquette for the E-mail Unlettered

Read a letter written a century or so ago, and you realize that the art of letter-writing has fallen upon pretty lean times. In those days, people set aside time to write, as entertainment, and the letters that flowed were long, thoughtful, literate, and intelligent. It was artful writing, with great swash signatures ("John Hancock"), all done in ink, using a bird feather as a pen, and unerasable ink. And no search/replace, and no block moves. And just about everyone did it.

Nowadays, we phone, and the art of letter-writing is a thing of the past. What is bedeviling many of us, however, is that a new technology—e-mail—is requiring that we think back and recall some of those letter-writing skills.

E-mail can take many forms—it is all the memos, reminders, chits, and notes we write that used to be sent through the U.S. mail or via interoffice mail, or call in by voice phone, that we now type into our computers. E-mail messages can be as long as a book or as short as a Post-It note. We tap out e-mail from remote offices, from hotel rooms and conference centers, from clients' offices.

For many of us, the day begins with writing a few such messages and ends with reading a handful of messages to us. It can be a way of swapping notes and reports within your company, from department to department. It can be a way to stay in touch while you're on the road, or working at home. It can be a way of communicating around the world, using services like MCI Mail, Genie, and CompuServe.

E-mail messages don't have to be flowery or erudite. But they are important—they say a lot about our values, our attention to detail, and the reputations of the organizations we represent. To help you bring your e-mail writing style up to snuff, here is a list of guidelines and tips.

1. **Sound human.** It doesn't matter how important the subject is, or how technical, or how important you are. Readable writing is simply talking, on paper. When in doubt about how to express something, write it the way you would say it. Use everyday language. Vary your sentence lengths. Be friendly. Use humor to break up the tension of what you have to say. E-mail is usually for your fellow team members, so show some team spirit. Say *ain't*. Do what you have to, to keep your readers from nodding off, or worse, wadding you up and discarding you.

2. **Don't be a noodle.** When my daughter was 4, she liked riddles, but she thought that any funny-sounding answer to any random question constituted a riddle. Her teacher explained riddles with a riddle:

Q. What is the difference between a needle and a noodle?
A. A needle has a point.

Never talk for the sake of talking. Say something! If you're just posting a message to remind people you exist, they may be moved to wonder why you exist. On-the-one-hand/on-the-other-hand posts go nowhere. Have courage, take a stand. State your conclusions at the beginning, not at the end. E-mail is no place for slowly unfolding drama.

3. **Ssshh!** Don't use ALL CAPS in any sustained way. They are OK for headlines or phrases that you might ordinarily underline or italicize. BUT TYPING LENGTHY STATEMENTS IN ALL CAPITAL LETTERS MAKES IT LOOK LIKE YOU ARE SHOUTING, and it is annoying. Alternatives to capitalizing when you wish to emphasize include bracketing emphases with underlines, _like this_, or with asterisks, like *this.* The rule should be to study the e-mail system you are on, to see what other people there use.

4. **Look sharp.** Ninety percent of good writing is clarity, and half of clarity is appearance. No one likes facing a long unbroken block of text characters. Your keyboard has an ENTER key—use it frequently. Put a blank line between paragraphs—it is a treat for your readers to see that each paragraph is really a separate thought. And it will help you to organize your own thinking. Use mini-headlines to summarize each paragraph that follows. If you have five points to make, why not number them as such, and indent each one. Or use bullets. Your reader's eyes will appreciate the visual organization.

In the old days people routinely wrote paragraphs 50 lines long. People had the time and attention spans to attack such monolithic paragraphs. No more. Today semicolons are the walking death of readability. Try to limit your paragraphs to four or five lines. Use white space—dashes—ellipses . . . they're all free.

5. **Be brief.** Posts don't have to fill a screen. Want to acknowledge a post from someone else? How about: *Good idea! Thanks! Way to go! Call me! You're fired!* You can be civilized without babbling. There's an old adage in show biz that is equally true in e-mail—leave 'em wanting more.

6. **Use macros, software-created shortcuts, that signal instantly what your memos are about.** Why not create a series of three macros that, at the touch of one key each, type the following prompts for you:

    (1) SUBJECT:
    (2) SUMMARY:
    (3) ACTION REQUIRED:

    If your name appears at the top, and your post is less than a screen long, don't sign with a macro ("Marilyn T. Anderson, Assistant Vice President-Environmental Services")—it's redundant. At the end of a longer post, however, when people may have forgotten who started the memo way back five screens earlier, it may be appropriate.

7. **Use your technology.** Use a memory-resident spell-checker or thesaurus if they help you avoid the embarrassment of misspelling a word or using one incorrectly.

    As often as possible, compose your messages off-line. Your regular word processor is much more powerful and easier to use than the tiny text editors used on most e-mail systems. You can do block moves, sorts, and all that deep-feature stuff that makes your memo shine—before going on-line. Grammar, style, and other usage software tools are fine. But they are no substitute to paying attention to what you say, and putting yourself in your intended reader's place. Best of all is showing the memo to another pair of eyes before saving it. If only to make sure you're using they're, there, and their right.

8. **Death to jargon and smart talk.** Jargon is language that you know, that is specific to your training or background, that other people may not know. If you sell medical instruments, your customers (physicians) may understand their jargon (medicine) but not yours (bioengineering). So put a lid on it. Smart talk—using pointless long words instead of simple understandable ones—is even worse. Saying *modification* instead of *change*, or *utilize* instead of *use*. *At this point in time* instead of *now*.

    Remember Al Haig ("Gentlemen, let me caveat that")? Talk English. If you're a blockhead, your reader will figure that out anyway, no matter how polysyllabic your vocabulary.

9. **Wait.** Just because you wrote your brilliant message from the very fires of your genius doesn't mean you can't set it aside for an hour or two before saving. Most e-mail systems allow you to compose messages off-line and upload them later. That may sound inefficient—it probably means printing out messages to you, and composing responses on a separate text editor like Q-Edit or Notepad. But the delay is time well-spent. It gives you the chance to say exactly what you want to say—and to re-read the message you're answering.

10. **Get a life.** Some executives and executives-to-be don't think they're being manly or managerial unless they fire off 50 messages each day. The psychology is that the mere presence of five daily messages in every employee's mail will convince them you are ten steps ahead of their every move. Lighten up! Smell the coffee, or smell the roses, or dump coffee on the roses and smell both.

Ambiguity is an inherent characteristic of language. Verbal communication can never be truly precise. Always, someone will take what someone else says "the wrong way." The trick is to put things as simply and directly as possible . . . to ask the other person if they understand correctly . . . and to keep paraphrasing until you're in complete agreement. Don't quit trying. Bad writing is its own worst enemy—it wastes time, corrodes the spirit of communication, puts your organization in a bad light, and undermines your own good reputation. Remember that your memo is not really for you—it's for that other person, who stands to benefit somehow from what you say. Why not say it in a way that maximizes that benefit?

JOIN THE CAMPAIGN AGAINST E-SLUDGE

Richard Fader of Passaic, New Jersey, writes with this predicament:

> Dear Mike,
> As a university professor I have been getting more and more messages on the Internet. I wouldn't mind if the messages were relevant to me, or required action on my part.
> At first I welcomed e-mail. It was direct, simple, and cheap. But lately it has been corrupted—by the same idiots that ruined the old system of paper memo routing.

I am talking about "cc-ing"—the habit of writing a memo, then adding a dozen names to the end. Using online services, it is simple to forward a message about the water cooler to a dozen people—or a thousand.

Some people maintain long mailing lists of people to include in their correspondence. They attach files to letters and letters to files—so that every day you peer into your e-mail box and see this dozen-eyed monster of riders, postscripts, and hangers-on all blinking at you, waiting to be read.

People who cc think that sending information to a dozen people instead of one makes their message more important. It is a way of showing off. Maybe they think you will be flattered to be included. But it is a huge bore. It was a terrible waste of paper and photocopying in the 1980s and it is a dreadful waste of time and bandwidth in the 1990s.

A recent event put me over the edge on this. I sent a memo to one individual that had made a slightly sensitive mention of another person. Well, that was dumb, but lo and behold, might you guess to whom my note was cc'd?

Michael, what can be done about these people? How can we get the word to them? Can technology come to the rescue?

Dear Professor Fader,

You know, for a fancy schmancy professor you sure worry about some eensy beensy things.

But I agree with you. One time I, Michael Finley, posted a message in a Usenet room bemoaning the clog and sprawl that was everywhere apparent. There is so much posting in some rooms that the entire contents can scroll by in as little as 48 hours.

My message was spotted by some group working to devise new Internet monitoring parameters to cope with the giant wave of e-sludge. They apprised me of their scheme and asked if I would like to be included in their private e-mail discussions on how to streamline e-mail.

You probably sense an ironic turn of events at this point, and rightly so. For every time I logged onto the Internet for the next few months, I was deluged with correspondence—10-20 pages per day—from this group seeking a better way.

E-sludge is like junk mail, only worse. Junk mail is easily identifiable—it is shiny and four-color, or it is in a brown envelope informing you you have won $40 million. Easy to spot, easy to discard. E-sludge, however, is from people you know, colleagues and associates whose goodwill you do not want to discard so lightly. The Internet and other services give users the option of creating a "kill file" of people you do not wish under any circumstances to exchange mail with.

This is great for fending off stalkers and dittoheads, but no help in dealing with customers and associates who think they are doing you a favor by including you on their daily perorations. They are more like door-to-door evangelists—you don't want to hurt their feelings, but you sure wish they would let you get back to your ball game.

Another possibility is to create a five- or six-line "signature" file—one that automatically ends every e-message you send—warning people that you don't care to be included in epistolary games of ring-around-the-rosy (a kids' game whose lyrics, I'm told, refer to the great bonfires of bodies conflagrated during the Black Death in Europe in the 14th Century). This is the equivalent of hanging a NO SOLICITING sign on your e-mailbox.

A good signature file mixes wit, whimsy, and a snippet of quotation or trivia. Mine is an earnest entreaty:

mfinley@skypoint.com

For the love of God, don't send me e-mail unless it has something to do with me.

You can come up with your own signature phrases, or you can use one of mine. There's the classical approach: "Into each life an occasional cc must drip—please don't drip yours into mine."

Pretend you're a grouch, and so take the onus of bad e-mail etiquette off them: "Give the precious gift of time—leave me the hell alone."

Or go mystical on them: "Silence is the great revelation—shut up and see."

If you're graphically inclined, Professor Fader, any of these can be crafted into beautiful four-color images suitable for uploading and downloading. You could make them look like those little sayings people have around their license plates, or a needlepoint sampler, or a kidnapper's note made of those cut-out letters from magazines.

Then, when e-mailers come a-tapping on the door to your burrow with a fresh load of sludge, they will see your signature, and steal quietly away.

But why wait until they show up at your door to spring it on them? Create a mailing list of everyone that has ever bothered you or might someday consider bothering you—then let 'em have it.

A preemptive attack of e-sludge, Professor Fader—that's what you need. It will teach them a lesson they will never forget. Do it for New Jersey. Do it for all of us.

CHAPTER ■ 4

When Bad Things Happen to Good Computers

The Importance of a Solid Repair Partnership

As equestrians of old relied on their trusted smithies, so must today's users of technology form strong bonds with professionals they trust

From the beginning of the personal computer revolution fifteen years ago, proponents have claimed ease of installation and repair as a primary feature. Old-fashioned mainframe computers required a white-jacketed team of on-call systems maintenance professionals to fine-tune and ease the big iron through its inevitable periods of adjustment.

By contrast, any intelligent user of desktop PCs could do anything that really needed doing: adding memory, installing expansion cards or peripherals, even diagnosing and solving run-of-the-mill operating problems (full hard disk, corrupted data, dead CMOS battery, etc.). You just unscrewed the screws in the back of the box, opened it up, fussed with a few wires and other things, and you were set.

Well, it was a crock fifteen years ago and it's still a crock. PCs and their components are modular in design; they are made of subcomponents (power supplies, hard drives, CD-ROMs, fax modems, etc.) that can't be fixed—only thrown out and replaced. A single chip may be all that's wrong with a fritzed modem. But chips are cheap; cheaper than labor, anyway. So the modem card is frisbeed onto the pile.

The most common user interventions can be grouped into four classes, according to difficulty. A skilled technician will tell you that most of these tasks are the same: you look at the manual, compare the factory settings with everything else you have in your system, and make

DYSFUNCTION
Paradox #4
The more open the architecture, the more you need a third-party repair team.

changes where there are conflicts. But unless you do this sort of thing a lot, you will never feel at home with it. The documentation is almost, but not quite, standard. The schematic drawing may predate the way the latest version of the peripheral looks. Jumpers, dipswitches, IRQs, interrupts, COM ports—it's enough to drive all but the techno natural to strong drink.

1. EASY

These are things just about anyone but a complete technophobe can do; yes, even worriers, people people, and dreamers.

- install Windows
- install most applications
- install a game port and joystick
- install an external modem or CD-ROM
- upgrade to the latest version of a program
- switch monitors
- install mouse and driver

2. MAYBE

Most pluggers, questers, and skeptics shouldn't have too much trouble with these tasks.

- install additional serial or parallel ports
- install a scanner
- install video or sound drivers to Windows
- replace or reassign a floppy drive
- snap in SIMM memory
- replace CMOS battery

3. UH OH

Getting into deeper water now. Earnest users may be able to tackle these jobs without assistance.

WHEN BAD THINGS HAPPEN TO GOOD COMPUTERS

- install an internal modem
- install a voicemail system
- replace hard disk
- install internal CD-ROM
- replace microprocessor
- install tape drive
- add chip memory
- install fax modem
- set up Internet gateway
- wire one computer to another to create a peer network

4. FORGET IT

These tasks are for techno naturals only; other types need not apply.

- install multimedia system
- add a second hard disk
- swap motherboards

"When in doubt, use brute force.

Ken Thompson, co-inventor of UNIX[1]

The most a typical barely competent user can do to keep a PC alive is to vacuum it out every couple of months, get rid of the sweaters it is knitting for you inside, massage the memory chips to make sure they are seated deep in their sockets, and tighten the various cables and connections. That's not much. It reminds me of the reason elevator makers install dummy buttons in automatic elevators: it's so users feel that, if anything goes wrong, at least they can push those buttons. It's something—an anxiety diminisher. And yet I have read 500-page do-it-yourself manuals whose actual fix-it wisdom could be reduced to "Watch out for dust and check your connections."

I have owned or had sole use of ten or eleven PCs in my life and have tried to fix or alter all of them. Looking back, I shake my head and wonder what I was thinking. Simple installation jobs that would have cost $30 in labor at the store ballooned until I was shelling out $100 or $150 to my repair crew to undo what I had undone.

It's so easy to make things much worse. You can inadvertently expose a laser printer drum to bright light and ruin it. You can unground an important connection.

WHAT YOU *CAN DO* YOURSELF

Add easy things. SIMMS memory strips are pretty easy to stick in. Video cards and mice are about as close to no-brainers as one can get. Phones, fax machines, copiers, and printers set up without much difficulty. Changing monitors is the closest thing we have today to true plug-and-play.

Examine those floppies. Floppy drives only last a couple of years under heavy use. Your drive may be going long before it starts to groan and skip. Flip open the metal sleeve on the 3½" floppies you use a lot—boot disks and such. Look on the surface that is exposed—friction rings are a sure sign that your drive is headed south.

Massage your unit. No, this is not what it sounds like. PCs generate heat, and the constant expansion and contraction of chips can loosen them right out of their sockets. They look fine. But when you pass over them with the soft part of your thumb, pressing them in, you hear these gratifying pops as they return to the proper position.

(Continued on page 81)

You can install one peripheral and create a conflict with a peripheral that you already had in there, so that neither one of them works. You can short out an expansion card or an entire motherboard with static electricity you've been storing in your carpet all winter.

You may object, "But, Mike, maybe you're a nitwit." I am, about hardware especially. But it isn't just me. I took an Internet e-mail poll of the dozen or so computer columnists I really respected, the most familiar names, and I asked them a single question about maintenance and repair. Here is the question and some of the answers:

Is there an aspect of everyday PC use (installing things, configuring your system, troubleshooting problems) that you find especially frustrating? What is it?

Where do I begin? Got a few hours and a handful of Prozac? If Dante were alive today he would have to create a new circle of Hell, this one known as the Windows General Protection Fault where sinners spend eternity in the 386enh section of their WIN.INI file wondering what "aperture-base=100" means.—David Churbuck, technology editor, *Forbes.*

The PC's resources (ports, DMA addresses, interrupts) are so limited that products step all over one another all the time.—Bill Machrone, *PC Magazine.*

Configuration problems are always the worst. I don't especially mind popping the top on a PC to get inside to stick a card in or mount a new hard drive. But I hate the IRQ/DMA-channel/memory starting address/memory exclude craziness. There has to be a better way (and is, of course: it's spelled M-a-c).—Jim Seymour, columnist for *PC Week* and *PC Magazine*.

See? If people who know what they're doing don't know what they are doing, is there any hope for you and me?

What we are left with is Paradox #4: "The More Open the Architecture, the More You Need a Third-Party Repair Team." But what makes a good repair partner, and how good is good?

LOOKING FOR MISTER GOODBUS

The machine looked like a putty-colored god when you first pulled it from its Styrofoam chrism. And for a whole two years it ran like a charm. Only today, when you booted it up and were greeted with stony silence, did you doubt.

Static-B-Gon. A quick cure for catastrophic bursts of electricity from one's fingertips is a 50% solution of Stay-Puff fabric softener in water, sprayed daily on the carpet.

Buy your PC from your repairman. Why not? The repair choice is ultimately more important than the store or brand choice. You may pay $200 more than you would at a store—low-volume repair shops can't match store prices. But you will have the repairman over a barrel. He sold you the machine, so he should have no excuses if he can't get it to work.

Check your cables. They do come loose from their connections. Worse, if you have been fiddling around inside, pins can be bent, and ribbons crimped. Printer cables outside the box tend to go bad at the connector.

Save the screws. Why? Oh, no special reason.

That doubt deepened when you phoned your retailer and got a disconnected notice, or saw in the fine print that your warranty had expired, or the salesperson said, "We don't service that make any more. Hey, Harvey, I got a guy on line one with a Model M7 that was working as recently as yesterday!"

Anyway, when it's time to "take it in," who do you take it in to? If you bought your system within ninety days, you can usually take it right back to the store or dealer for repair. If you bought an extended service

"If technology is so good for us, why haven't we all benefited from it? If computers are more efficient in running businesses, why aren't employees paid more? Why are computers used to constrict and define our lives, instead of enhancing them? Why are so many computer systems used to tighten control and increase surveillance rather than to expand personal freedom?

As computer technology eliminates employment, where are the new jobs coming from? Why have so few efforts been made to explain computer technology to ordinary people? Why do governments and the media accept as an article of faith that technological innovation means progress? Why do technocrats use incomprehensible language to describe technology?"

Ian Reinecke[2]

contract beyond ninety days, you (the First Party) can take it to the warranty repair people (the Second Party). If you're completely on your own, you can still take it to the Second Party, or you can do what growing numbers of computer owners do—find a Third Party repair outfit. Mr. Goodbus.

Finding Mr. Goodbus—one you can really trust—is not easy. Local computer tabloids abound with listings of computer repair companies, much as the Yellow Pages abound with auto mechanics. (Scads of people would still be drifting aimlessly through life had they not picked up a matchbook at a ham radio swap meet asking the technological question: Can You Switch These COM Addresses to the Proper IRQ Interrupts and Hex Locations?) The best way to locate a good one is to ask around. Get on a bulletin board (if your system still allows you to), and ask who people have been satisfied with. Within 24 hours you'll have the equivalent of $12,000 worth of focus group research, and two or three phone numbers.

You will find that they are not all the same. After fifteen years the computer repair business is still in early adolescence, rather like auto mechanics at the turn of the century, where former liverymen needed to adapt to technologies as different as steam and gasoline. As with car mechanics, computer mechanics are all over the board in terms of reliability, quality of work, pricing, customer commitment, and business practices.

There are five formal classes of repair entities:

1. **The hole in the wall,** formed by a couple of guys both named Allen. They have Star Trek Voyager posters on their walls, and the place is a mess of boxes and odd parts lying around. They know no more than you, and have no way of finding out, either. They may make an eccentric change that will void warranties. But they are nearby and they are pretty cheap. Sometimes they will take hours to check something out and not charge you for the time, because your problem has engaged their curiosity. Call them "The Revenge of the Nerds."

2. **The small professional repair company** that also does training and network installations. They advertise in the local computer rag and go by a name like UpComp or CompuTime or TechMatic. They work ridiculous hours, survive on Cheetohs, bite their tongues when hearing users describe their usage patterns. They wish they had more big corporate customers, but they are stuck with you instead.

3. **The authorized regional repair office** for a major retailer. This is where the corporate customers flock to. These folks have a good thing going with their big bucks strategic ally, but you wouldn't know it. Service is impersonal, prices high, and things hardly ever fall under warranty.

4. **The back room of a store.** Overworked and underpaid, with incredible turnover, these folks are an inexpensive solution to the problem of merchandise rushed to market and manuals rushed into print even faster. Can you say Heavy Turnover?

5. **A mail order shop;** you pack up your system and ship it to them. They are often located next to a large swamp. After a month you just hope you see your stuff again; if it is even halfway fixed, that is gravy.

Watching a computer repair person is such a different experience from opening the box up yourself and attacking things with a bandsaw. I stood behind Chuck, my repair guy, one afternoon (right under the "LABOR $20/HR—$40 IF YOU HELP" sign), and it was instructive

WHAT TO LOOK FOR IN A REPAIR TEAM

Techno mystique. The air of mystery that some technoids like to surround themselves in. A hand-me-down from the days of the sacerdotal cyberneticist. You want as little of this as possible.

Hunger. If your team is accustomed to dealing with Fortune 500 customers and you are a small business, they aren't likely to bend over too far backward for you. Find someone your own size, who understands problems at your level and within your budget.

English-speaking. As opposed to not speaking at all. You want a repair team that knows how to listen and what to say to put you at ease: how long it will take, how much it will cost, what you should do in the meantime.

Long-term. Anyone can fix a flat tire. What you want is someone who will be there for you when true disaster strikes, and between disasters.

Emotionally stable. Some techies wince when coming in contact with customers. Customers whine, complain, curse, declaim. They are in dire straits and may say something very unkind. You want a repair team with a thick skin and a forgiving heart.

Preventive-minded. A stitch in time . . .

seeing how he manhandled the chips and connections, almost like a masseur, pressing each with his thumbs to restore close fit. He was at home with the circuitry, to a degree I could only dream of. A good repair partner brings that level of hands-on craftsmanship to the work.

Chuck's shop doesn't really fix stuff. For the most part, computer hardware seldom breaks. Chips occasionally burn out, and peripherals get fried by dry weather and static electricity. Floppies frazzle after a couple of years of heavy grinding. Laptops generate lots of heat with little ventilation, causing component failure. Power supplies burn out, especially if your local electricity has lots of hiccups in it. Monitors are rugged—if they fail it's usually in the first month and are covered by warranty; otherwise they are usually good for five years. Laser printers wear out very slowly; the bigger problem is obstructions—paper, dust, label jams, and using the wrong grade of toner.

What Chuck's shop does do is switch stuff. They take out the offending or underpowered unit, and put in a healthy or more powerful one. They add stuff to your PC. In addition, most shops resell, broker, evaluate, appraise, train, and consult. Perhaps consult is the most operative term of the bunch, since it gets at the real dynamic that exists between first and third parties. Sometimes people want to upgrade but aren't sure what to do—switch motherboards, extend memory, install a speed-up card or new fixed disk. Mr. Goodbus is supposed to be able to point you in the right direction. Unlike straight retailers, he won't be pushing what's on sale that week. He'll be listening to your needs and helping untangle the possibilities.

It is sometimes said of car mechanics that they can be the customer's best friend or worst enemy. It's equally true of Mr. Goodbus. Repair and maintenance work is all about taking heat. Technology is absolutely tied to people's ability to earn a livelihood and, in some cases, to function as human beings. People not only want the job done right, and quick, but they want absolute confidence that the machines will continue to work, far into the future.

Have you had this happen with your car? You have your carburetor fixed, and on the way home from the shop, your right rear wheel falls off. Why does the wheel fall off? Did the fellow at the garage loosen the lug nuts? Is it some plot to keep your jalopy on the rack?

The same thing happens with computers.

Because they were working on your computer just before you set it back up, repair partners find themselves in an awkward position. An individual can buy a new hard disk, and within a week it will fail. You can replace that hard disk and within another week it will fail. By that time the customer is blowing lava from his nostrils. And what can the repair person say. "Gee, if that isn't the darnedest thing." And so it is.

I asked Chuck if two catastrophes following upon the heels of one another might not suggest operator error of some sort? "You can think it," Chuck said gravely, "but you don't dare say it." The clever repair partner tiptoes around assigning blame.

Another dicey area is helping customers make the fix/forget decision. What does one do with a Hewlett-Packard InkJet printer that, after six and a half years of blissful operation, coughs blood and dies? The electronics are shot. The nozzles are all fused. A new machine of the same technology type costs about $600; the repair will cost almost that much. What does the considerate repair person do?

"Whatever makes the customer happy," Chuck said. "If having the old printer up and running again will do that, then that's what we do." If the time has come for a change, and the customer agrees, then you upgrade. If you hate the printer and you always did, it would be pretty stupid to fetch it back from the grave.

Laptops mean special repair problems

Downtime sends a shudder through every corporate office and can be even more perplexing to people on the road. The first time our laptop goes down, it is a shock.

The catalog of complaints about laptops and notebooks are the same you hear about desktop models—hard disk problems, floppy disk problems, and display failures. But problems occur more frequently, and for good reasons. Usually the causes have to do with the ways people use their laptops. Laptops suffer a lot more abuse than desktop machines. They get moved around a lot, they experience extreme temperature changes, from 20 below to 110 above. Every time you open one up you stretch cables. Contacts go bad. Disk drives are touchier because, with no fan to cool the system down, there is less heat dissipation.

(Continued on page 87)

It's a happiness thing. Sometimes Mr. Goodbus has to swallow hard and not charge Mr. Customer for work he did. Maybe Mr. Customer had Mr. Goodbus waste time testing the wrong peripheral. Maybe Mr. Goodbus was chasing a problem down a blind alley. Maybe Mr. Goodbus was displaying splendid initiative that he was not, alas, authorized to display.

Sometimes Ms. Customer takes 30 days to pay her bill. Sometimes 120 days comes and goes. (This seems especially true when Ms. Customer is also Ms. Lawyer.) Ms. Customer is not always Ms. Perfect, and yet she is always right, just by dint of being Ms. Customer.

If you secure a good repair partner, cultivate him or her. I invited mine out for hamburgers. It was one of those PC repairman places, out along the strip. Nothing fancy, like plates. Just you, your mouth, and a drippy sandwich.

One other thing: don't ask about their kids. If they are any good at all, they haven't seen them in days.

Diary of a repair

Maintaining a good relationship with your repair partner is essential to maintaining a semblance of technological mental health. The problem is that the difficulties of the technology contrive to strain even the best relationship, as I found out when my hard drive died.

August 15 Dear diary, I am very pleased with a purchase I made today. My old tape backup just wasn't big enough for the hard drive I bought last month, so I sprang for a 240 megabyte Colorado drive, for $295—$50 less than I paid for a drive half that size three years ago! I tell you, we are living in glorious times. I bought it from my regular repairman, Chuck.

Chuck and I have known each other for about eight years. That's almost a century in computer time. We've done lots of business in that time—systems, components, repairs, the works. This system is just what I need to complement that new hard drive. I have terrific confidence in Chuck. He's down to earth, smart, and he appreciates that I need to be up and running. Sure is a good feeling, having him on the team.

> As a rule, laptops are better engineered and constructed than desktop machines. But after 1,000 kicks and jostles, something inside those boxes is bound to give. Laptops are also harder to work on. Just cracking open a laptop is a challenge for first-timers. Likewise, they take longer to reassemble when you are done. Most repair people will tell you stories of the laptop they could fix, but had a dickens of a time reassembling—psychotically small screws and lots of them, cables too short by a fraction of an inch, no room to wiggle fingers around in. And they are more expensive. Laptop parts typically cost 150 to 200 percent what their desktop equivalents cost.

August 16 Dear diary, bad news. This morning when I booted up, my new hard disk made this gruesome sound, like broken glass being chewed by a garbage disposal. Two seconds later, the video fluttered and failed. I knew I was in big trouble and took it in to Chuck. The news was worse than I thought. My hard drive was destroyed. The power supply, a hefty 250-watt job: dead. Worst of all, the motherboard itself was knocked out of commission.

It was a disaster, and the thoughts going through my head— wipeout, wipeout, money, deadlines, help!—were very painful to me. My PC's warranty expired months before—I was vulnerable to a huge hit, perhaps as much as $2,000. Chuck suggested we sleep on the problem and try to come up with a solution. I drove home soberly, without my computer.

1654. The slide rule wars heat up yet again with the unveiling of the first rectilinear, "sliding" slide rule at Comdex 1654, in Rouen. This basic device, created by one Robert Bissaker, was to be the workhorse of scientific calculating till the invention of the pocket calculator three hundred years later.

1623. Wilhelm Schickard, described as a polymath, is a language wizard, a true combination right/left-brain renaissance man, with facility in both science and the arts. His "Calculating Clock" is the first true mechanical calculator. It incorporates Napier's logarithms onto rotating cylinders. One is commissioned by the great astronomer Johannes Kepler, but it is destroyed in a fire before it can be delivered.

(Continued on page 89)

August 17 I woke up this morning with the realization that of course the problem was the tape drive I had installed four days earlier. The last thing I did before powering down was back up the hard disk. Then, in the morning, kaboom.

I called Chuck and told him the problem had to be with the tape drive—his damn tape drive had trashed my entire computer! Chuck resisted the idea. He suggested it might be the power line in the house. I live and work in an old house, but the lights don't flicker, and we don't lose power often. Nothing else in the house was affected that night. I am beginning to spin scenarios in my mind in which I prove beyond a doubt that his tape drive wrecked my system. In my mind I am rolling these metal ball bearings over and over.

August 21 I am going crazy trying to work on my lousy little laptop. The screen is terrible, the keyboard stinks, and its 25 MHz 386 speed is something from *The Land Time Forgot.* I am running DOS applications, for crying out loud. I called Chuck to ask how the computer is coming. He says he wants to lend me a motherboard to get me by until mine is fixed. Sounds great to me.

August 22 Chuck sold me a new power supply and hard disk and is lending me a new 66-DX2 MHz 486 motherboard. But it only has 4 megs of memory. "You'll have to limp along like this for a few days," he said. "Maybe you can write an article about that." No problem, I said—what do I need 16 megs of memory for? (I forgot about

QuarkXPress.) I also had Chuck replace the killer tape drive with another brand. Chuck's full bill came to $675. And we still hadn't resolved the issue of who would pay for fixing the motherboard.

September 2 It's funny how hard it is to run a computer with only 4 megs of RAM. WordPerfect for DOS creeps along like maple syrup in March. There's not enough memory to put two big programs up at once, using Desqview. The print buffer is small, so printing is slow, and you're better off not printing something while running another program. Things are taking me longer to do.

September 4 Chuck called. He said his shop can't figure out what happened to my motherboard, or fix it, so they're sending it across town to a shop that specializes in that make of computer. They promised to fix it for $150 in 5-8 days.

September 13 I called Chuck and asked what happened to my motherboard. He said he will call the authorized repair center and find out what happened. The leaves have started to fall in the backyard. I look in the mirror and I seem—gray.

1642. Blaise Pascal is the first computer superstar. His "Pascaline" machine, built to help his lawyer dad handle tax accounts, is the first true adding machine. Pascal is a scientific, philosophical, and literary prodigy. He is also religious to the point of self-flagellation. His Pascaline is a set of interlocking cogs and wheels that adds sums when people dial the numbers they wish to add. The result is displayed in the windows. Only fifty Pascalines are ever made because clerks and accountants, ever the avatars of progress, fear the gadgets will eliminate their professions. Pascal dies at the young age of 39 of stomach cancer, one of the great what-if characters in world history— what might he have achieved had he lived a normal term?

September 16 Chuck says the authorized repair center told him the motherboard is unfixable, and he's upset that they charged him $20 to tell him that. "I am not going to pay that," he fumes. I don't tell him that I don't care what he pays or doesn't pay—I just want my computer back, and my 16 megabytes.

September 24 I called Chuck today and told him I was sick of the long wait. He said he had good news—he shipped my motherboard off to the manufacturer, in Chicago. They promised to fix the motherboard in a week and get it back to me.

down—Inoperative, as in "The up escalator is down."

doorstop—Any machine larger than a Scotch tape dispenser that has outlived its usefulness.

floating point—A kind of notation that lets you express a number as a product of a mantissa and a base number raised to a certain power. This kind of arithmetic allows computers to work with very large and very small numbers by reducing the number of required digits. Floating point arithmetic was where the Pentium had all its problems.

flop—A measurement of floating-point calculations per second. Used to compare computing speeds of powerful computers.

"I know you've been waiting, and I know you're impatient," Chuck told me. "But I'm going to make this worth your while. It won't cost you much—maybe $150—and I'm going to do something nice for you, maybe upgrade your memory to 20 megs." I said that would be great, but hurry—I was not getting my work done at my usual rate, and computer frustration was part of that.

I thought I saw a few stray snowflakes today.

October 1 Unbelievable—my new power supply, replaced five weeks ago—died today! I took it in to Chuck and looked at him ominously while he replaced the unit. At least this was on warranty.

The people at the insurance office next to Chuck's shop know me by sight now. We waved.

October 4 Day 48 of the computer hostage crisis. I was going to call Chuck but I changed my mind. I am ticked off that no one has gotten back to me about my motherboard, but I don't want to get into a fight with him on the phone.

October 5 Couldn't help myself. I called Chuck, and we went around and around. Chuck says he is looking out for me. I just want my motherboard back. He said he would call the factory and find out where it is and get back to me that day.

October 7 Still waiting for word from Chuck. I know those guys are busy, and I know they're not making money on me on this job, and I know they're sick of my calling—but dammit, it's been 52 days!

October 9 I'm calling every day now. In a slightly singsong voice, Chuck says, "Yes, Mike, we're trying to find your motherboard.

They told us it was in transit, then they told us it was lost, then they said they lost the BIOS chips. I'll get back to you the instant I find out. Promise."

October 10 Chuck is taking my side now. "Mike, I'm as fed up with this as you are. I'm going to write off the whole problem as a loss and charge it to the manufacturer somehow. I'm not sure how, but I'll do it."

In a depressed monotone, I replied, "Sounds great, Chuck. I'm really excited."

But I'm not. I don't care any more. I'm like the genie in the lamp. For 10,000 years I wanted to reward whoever freed me. But now I've gone evil from the long wait. Whoever pulls the cork now is gonna die.

October 11 Chuck says my old motherboard was found and is being shipped to the Twin Cities by truck. It will be here Monday and I can get set up again. Great.

October 14 I called and asked if my motherboard had arrived. It hadn't. When might it arrive, I asked. Friday, Chuck told me.

October 21 Chuck says the motherboard is in. Hallelujah.

October 23 Something came in, all right, but it's not my motherboard. The factory finally declared it was unfixable—as two previous parties had. So they shipped the BIOS chips back. Turns out that this BIOS is obsolete, the company doesn't make it any more, so it had to be plucked from my old dead motherboard—hence the three-week delay.

"For a list of the ways technology has failed to improve the quality of life, press 3."[3]

This morning I brought in the computer with the temporary motherboard in it, had Chuck put in the new motherboard, along with a RAM upgrade to 16 megs. When I came to pick it up in the afternoon, I found that no RAM upgrade was made—Chuck didn't have the chips he'd been promising me for over a month.

So—I blew. I stomped about his office for several minutes, muttering, salivating, chronicling my frustrations getting back on-line. I was almost crying. Even I could sense how unpleasant I was being, and I can't usually do that. I remember using the phrases "the last straw" and "sixty-five days" several times.

Finally, Chuck glowered at me and I stopped pacing. "Listen," he said. "I want to make sure you're up and running, without problems.

When we're sure that you're OK, I'll personally come to your house and install the memory."

I didn't believe him. My confidence was in shreds. But I had used up my whining quota for the week, so I packed up the computer and drove it home.

October 27 Having my computer back and running, and able to run a zillion programs simultaneously once again, has brightened my outlook considerably. The hate lines over my eyes are starting to smooth out.

But I worry. About the high cost of repairs. Who can afford a $1,500 repair, at the drop of a hat, and when it's done not even know what happened exactly? I never found out what caused my motherboard to fail. I insisted a bad tape drive somehow fried the guts of my machine. To Chuck that was ridiculous—yet he had no better idea to offer.

"It's like with your car," he told me. "You get something fixed, and then, for some odd reason, something else breaks right away. Of course it was the mechanic's fault, in your mind. But the mechanic knows he didn't do anything that could have caused that failure. It's just a coincidence, but it can drive you crazy.

"Same with your computer. You say the problem was the tape drive. Maybe so. In my mind, it could just as easily have been the banging the computer took when you transported it back and forth, or unreliable power in your house. I don't think we'll ever know. Finding out why is just too expensive."

October 30 I'm left with an uneasy sense about what it means to own a computer. Unless owners have a service contract or extended warranty, they are at the mercy of unfathomable technological glitches, overnight obsolescence, and a parts-and-service infrastructure that can be incredibly inefficient.

And all we have to combat this threat may be a repairman we think we can trust and the limited reservoirs of our own personal charm.

I shouldn't have gotten sore at Chuck. He was just trying to help. But circumstances ganged up on me, and the repair wound up taking 65 days. Chuck didn't make a dime. He never charged me for his time and only charged me what he paid for parts—$275. He picked up all the freight and telephone costs himself.

And yet, I was rankled. Like Marlon Brando told Rod Steiger in *On the Waterfront*—his job was to take care of me. To keep a sharp lookout for problems, and head them off at the pass when possible. But of course, what could Steiger do? Life was tough on the waterfront. And life is tough on the computer repair front, too.

Though tested to the max by this ordeal, ours is a good relationship, and I would be foolish to wad it up and throw it away because this one project slipped away. I'm going to stick with Chuck, and I hope he sticks with me.

Computers come and go, but a repair partner who will put up with you while you put up with him is hard to find.

CHAPTER ■ 5

How Technology Is Turning the Office Upside Down

And How We Can Stay Upright

Rising high above our desktops we glimpse the dizzying "Big Picture," in which we are but hapless pawns in a grand scheme of productivity, then swoop down to the scene of our own waste

If technology makes us so productive, how come we're not rich? It's a long story, that takes us far from our desktops and back into time.

Back when the digital computer was invented during World War II—a clicking, blinking mainframe the size of a house—no one was thinking about user happiness or its counterpart, techno madness. There was a war to be won, codes to be cracked, a world to be saved.

Likewise, when your company installed its first centralized computing system, a Digital or IBM or Hewlett-Packard minicomputer, they weren't trying to put smiles on people's faces, either. They were seeking to obtain an advantage over their competitors. Office automation didn't sound too pleasant, but it was a strategic route to survival.

When you yourself made the crossing from occasionally accessing the company computer to having a desktop PC all your own to play with, with your own little processor in there, even you weren't thinking about happiness. You focused on the things you could do that you couldn't do before. That dream of enhanced productivity was your substitute happiness.

So we keep buying new computers, learning how to use them, and using them, and then buying new ones again. It is seldom that we stop, look in the mirror, and wonder whether happiness will ever enter the picture. And if it doesn't, that's pretty sad.

Technology at its cruelest is a mill that chews people up and spits out the bones. No matter how augmented you are, or how productive you get, it never seems to be enough.

TOIL
Paradox #5

The technology-rich get richer, and the rest get buried.

THE PRODUCTIVITY PARADOX

The U.S. is the most office-automated country in the world. We have twice as many computers per worker as Japan, the next most computerized nation. Techno craziness should be stamped: *Made right here in the U.S.A.* Statistically, we also lead the world in productivity. But you would think, with all that augmentation going on, we would be even more productive. Our rate of productivity growth has been falling for years, and other countries have overtaken us. So what's the deal?

From 1950 to 1965, our average business productivity grew at a sizzling 3 percent. From 1965 to 1973, the rate dropped to a still commanding 2 percent. Since 1973, it's slowed even more, to 1 percent.

We're still top dog worldwide, productivitywise. We lead the world in gross domestic product and in output per hour per manufacturing worker, with Canada, Japan, France, and Germany substantially behind us. But as the rate of productivity declines, the chances of being overtaken, and soon, are pretty good.

Here's the kicker: this drooping in the rate of productivity exactly parallels the blossoming of desktop computers. It is a very weird paradox, because if computers promise anything, it's raw productivity. Surely a secretary using WordPerfect is more productive than a typist from the generation preceding him? Surely an engineer running AutoCAD is piling up drawings and schematics far faster than her predecessor at the drawing board?

---

fried—Down for the duration.

glitch—from the Yiddish *glitchen*, meaning to skid or slide.

glork—The sound a user makes involuntarily when taken by surprise. It begins in the back of the throat, rises, pirouettes, then tumbles out the nose.

The paradox can be explained, and once it is, we can breathe a bit easier about the alarming productivity statistics we keep hearing. First of all, what is this thing we call productivity? Textbooks describe it with a simple equation:

$$P = \frac{\text{OUTPUT ACHIEVED}}{\text{RESOURCES USED}}$$

Or, verbosely: Productivity equals the sum of all goods and services produced, divided by the sum of all the capital, manpower, materials, machines, land, and buildings that were necessary for the production process.

Those are heavy-duty equations. Translated to the national level, you picture a country in which experts know exactly what each individual's output is, as if we all have the tallyman tally our bananas before quitting time each day.

The problem is that we are not in the banana business. In the old days, when manufacturing and agriculture were the linchpins of the American economy, tallying bananas made sense. But with the rise of the service economy, all the metrics have gone to hell.

How do you measure the productivity of a designer? His hourly output may be minuscule—and yet his new product may be what saves his company in any given year. How do you measure a CEO's productivity? What is her "product"?

Productivity has become so much more than pieceworkers rolling new product out to the truck dock, but the measurements that cause us such grief take no account of this. Consider the "liability" half of the verbose definition above. These things are all lumped in as overhead: the creativity of managers, researchers, designers, planners. If they are doing their jobs well, they are much more than overhead—they are the soul of your company, the wellspring of customer satisfaction.

There are many who feel that the entire concept of productivity is obsolete. It doesn't matter how many bananas you tally at day's end if the market has no use for bananas, or puts low value on them, or your bananas taste like camel cud. Value derives not from output (what you make) but from intake (whether your customer chooses to buy it).

And here we come to the true bounty that computers have yielded—value adding. The textbook formula for productivity is rooted in a very outdated way of measuring industrial success, Frederick Taylor's principles of scientific management. It's a fine way to compare productivity between an assembly plant in Burma and an assembly plant in Nicaragua, where nearly every worker is engaged in a routine, measurable task.

But as soon as computers come into the picture, the old metrics start to fall apart. The worker of today, in this country, is just as likely to be a knowledge worker as a manual laborer. The measurements that work for manual labor—pieces turned out per hour or per dollar of wage—simply don't work when applied to managers, engineers, designers—anyone who has been freed by computers to think, evaluate, and decide.

Think of how computers have changed the way so many functions in industry work. The field of accounting today is finally a profession. It's gone way beyond doing the books and taxes and is now involved in every dimension of management consulting, plus a hundred value-adding subspecialties. Take away Lotus 123, Quattro Pro, and Excel, however, and they are a knot of unaugmented Bob Cratchits again, perched on stools and scratching in ledgers.

Who Has the Computers?

We do. At year's end 1993, this was how the world's 173 million computers were distributed. Note the gap between #1 and #2. Note the status of Russia and China.[1]

Country	Number of computers (in millions)
USA	74
Japan	12.2
Germany	10.4
United Kingdom	9.4
France	7.4
Canada	5.2
Italy	4.4
Australia	3.4
Spain	3.1
Netherlands	2.1
S. Korea	1.7
Mexico	1.6
Taiwan	1.6
Sweden	1.3
Belgium	1.2
Russia	1.2
China	1.2
Brazil	1.1

Pat the Accountant

Let's illustrate how the value—not the volume—of work explodes when hardware and software are applied to a simple business function. Imagine your name is Pat, and this is your career to date:

FOUR NOT ESPECIALLY PRESCIENT REMARKS[2]

"It would appear that we have reached the limits of what it is possible to achieve with computer technology, although one should be careful with such statements, as they tend to sound pretty silly in five years."

John Von Neumann, c. 1949

"There is no reason for any individual to have a computer in their home."

Ken Olsen, CEO,
Digital Equipment, 1977

"Inventions reached their limit long ago, and I see no hope for further development."

Julius Frontinus,
1st century A.D.

"I can see the time when every city will have one."

*An American mayor's
reaction to the news of the
invention of the telephone*

1970 You graduate from the University of Minnesota with a degree in accounting. You get a job with a regional accounting firm, doing corporate tax work. Your technology is a Burroughs adding machine. Somewhere on the 12th floor is an IBM mainframe. Your take-home pay that first year, $16,500. You work, on average, 50-hour weeks, with one week off. April is hell on earth.

1985 You are a big success. You are president of a smaller, 40-person firm, running the business off a DEC VAX system. Of your workforce, 17 are professionals, doing tax work, and 23 are support staff—managing clerical chores, bookkeeping, filing, billing, and marketing. Three of the younger accountants are excited about a new program, VisiCalc, that runs on a little machine called an Apple II. They don't even upload to the mini system anymore. You've got more vacation time now—three weeks—but still pulling long hours. Annual salary: $110,000.

1995 How could so much have happened in ten years? You sold your tax firm and set up an office of your own, in an old farmhouse by a lake. You have two junior associates that you never see—they telecommute, and you pass work using a local area network. You affiliate with a half dozen other small firms, in New York, Toronto, Buenos Aires, and Singapore. Your entire company runs off a global network of PCs, using Lotus Notes and the Lotus SmartSuite of office applications—1-2-3, Ami Pro, and Freelance Graphics for Windows. You retain an office manager, who doubles as system administrator for the network. No secretaries, no file clerks, no bookkeepers—the office manager handles all that, using PC software and other office automation. Both your OUTPUT ACHIEVED and your RESOURCES USED have changed drastically, making hash of the old productivity. You're not even doing tax work any more, which you now admit you hated all along. Your firm is a brain trust, consulting on a handful of complementary matters—strategic planning, quality management, information services, and process reengineering. There's lots more baloney to talk about, and it's fun. You figure you are finally down to a 35-hour work week. Annual take-home pay—$185,000. And you have a boat.

Now, that's a success story, with no discernible techno craziness. Not every banana picker graduates to superstar consultant, but it happens. The on-paper productivity of the main character in it has not changed significantly over the 25-year period. And yet everything that means anything has changed. It's the productivity metric that's no dang good.

It was value that raised the salary of our hypothetical accountant, Pat, from $7.30 per hour in 1970 to $96.30 per hour 25 years later. A new productivity metric, to be comprehensible, will have to somehow deal with value, quality, and new processes for making things. If we are lucky, some clever

1673. Gottfried von Leibniz is a philosopher (he coins the phrase "best of all possible worlds," meaning ours) and a mathematician on a par with Isaac Newton (they both invented calculus, more or less simultaneously). He also creates an advanced calculating machine, "The Leibniz Wheel," that uses a cylinder of stepped teeth to do what the Pascaline can not—subtract, multiply, and divide. Leibniz's invention caps a whirlwind period in the history of computing mechanics—perhaps the greatest ever. The future may look back on their gearwheels and cranks and smirk. But hey—they did it without Lotus 1-2-3, without AutoCAD to flesh out their drawings, and without CompuServe to solicit overnight feedback on.

1804. Jacquard's Loom. This was a weaving machine, made by Joseph Marie Jacquard (after whom "Jacquard prints" are still named) that programmed design instructions to itself. The cards containing the programs survived in concept all the way through to the card instructions fed to mainframe computers in the 1960s.[46]

(Continued on page 100)

1822. The Difference Engine. The first true computing machine, this idea never came to fruition. Neither did the idea that replaced it, Babbage's Analytical Engine. But they were both startlingly ambitious—1940s-style computing machines made along the lines of 1820s-style hard metal manufacturing, using old-fashioned gear-driven mechanics. These were all-purpose machines, not the single-purpose computers (code-cracking, tide-charting) developed in the 1930s and '40s. It needed an engine with the power of a steam locomotive to make it run, at least on paper. Years later, a working model of the Difference Engine was built by Swedish inventor Georg Scheutz. English mathematician Charles Babbage was a complete failure in his own life, but he goes into the books as one of the great visionaries of all time.

---

person somewhere is creating a better metric even as we speak, involving customers retained, days late, proportion of work needing re-doing, inventory turns, complaints handled, etc. Manufacturing long ago realized that productivity apart from quality is meaningless; it's time the rest of us followed suit.

Maybe the best way to resolve anxieties about productivity ("Are we working hard enough? Can we compete?") is to accept that this is just the way Americans are. We love to throw ourselves at machinery. We end up creating some great numbers. But we know in our hearts that we do it because it is our national obsession. We work hard, play hard, waste lots of time at the PC doing things that don't help "the enterprise" one bit. Whether we are pluggers or dreamers, we are a very kinetic people.

The real reason we have more computers than other countries is that they suit us.

WHO KNOWS WHERE THE PRODUCTIVITY GAINS GO?

In a single hour the modern exponentiated office worker can churn out 50 times the paperwork that he or she could produce in an entire day 20 years ago. And the work will look immaculate, be more persuasive, and contain more and more reliable information.

But by year's end most of us experience only modest productivity gains. The time-savings disappears somehow. What prevents us from maintaining our incredible potential pace?

I set out to identify where the time goes. I crisscrossed this great land, peering over people's shoulders on the job, sneaking and snooping to learn what was undercutting their output. And came up with some very interesting categories of waste. Here are just the top ten:

- **Compulsion.** Some tasks engage us disproportionately to their importance. The best examples are the games that come with Windows. Many top business leaders go around at night, using the old-fashioned SneakerNet system, deleting these games from employees' hard disks. It is not that they are great games. They aren't. But God help us, many are unable to quit a session of Windows Solitaire till we win that one game. And then we want to win a second to prove it wasn't a fluke.
- **Self-defense.** The cyber regions have unfriendly skies. The casual visitor to UseNet newsgroups on the Internet may make the fatal mistake of posting inappropriately in a key room, like posting an original post in **alt.best-of-internet**. That is a severe no-no; the room is a digest of posts nominated from other groups. You will get fifteen officious e-mail messages from complete strangers telling you in the language of a 15-year-old what an inconsiderate impersonator of a human being you are. You feel you have no option except to reply forcefully to each, and the afternoon is soon shot.
- **Inquiry.** Your PC is an instrument of learning, and you have no trouble justifying time spent in pursuit of truth. Never mind that the truth you seek is what key combinations toggle Omniscient Mode in Cosmo's Cosmic Adventure. (Hit G, for God.)
- **Cosmetics.** In the earthy argot of today's computerists, pour the tea or put down the pot. How often we find ourselves at the crucial moment when a document is ready to print, and we think, "Hey, I'll bet I could really pretty that proposal up with a two-color border and a couple of daffodils." If we had desktop publishing 50 years ago, we would still be at war.
- **Ecology.** As natural as the newbie's impulse to defend himself against veteran newsgroup posters is the impulse of the grizzled net veteran to mount full-scale persecutions of newbies. The beginners will call you cruel, misanthropic, a big meanie. Tut tut, you reply, I am merely culling the herd.
- **Interior decoration.** Somewhere in your array of screen savers, wallpaper patterns, system fonts, and color schemes, there is a

combination that will overcome the weaknesses of your monitor, ease eyestrain forever, and enable you to work for 12 hours at a stretch. But first, you have to try out each of the 3.5 kajillion combinations.

- **Economy.** The committed optimizer is on a ceaseless quest for shortcuts. Why settle for a three-click series of mouse clicks to open and close a file, taking four full seconds, when with a couple of hours of batch-file programming, you can create a keyboard macro that achieves the same feat in three seconds?

- **Ennui.** Waiting two whole minutes for the Mosaic transmission of a .BMP graphic of asteroids striking the surface of Jupiter. Standing in the middle of an empty superstore for twenty minutes trying to get the attention of a salesperson. Listening to "Muskrat Love" while waiting for your call to advance in the tech support queue. There are moments in every computer user's life when time stands still. What you wouldn't give for a stick of gum about then.

- **Idleness.** You wonder why advertisers ask for information about prospective customers on those inquiry cards in the back of *PC Magazine.* Is it likely that anyone with the authority to make a buy decision for an entire company is flipping languidly through the marketplace section of a 600-page magazine? I guess it is.

- **Stupidity.** The mother of all time devourers. Doing things that add no value, and that you wouldn't have to do if you'd used your head. Replacing vital data you were too busy to back up. Retyping documents you were too lazy to digitize. Recreating entire projects because you didn't think anyone around you was dumb enough to trip over the power cord.

And these ten points are just the tip of the iceberg. Every moment we are not doing what the books say, and adding value to the customer, we are wasting time, and America's handhold on the merry-go-round ring of global competitiveness becomes that much more tenuous. Once gone, that moment can never be recalled.

Fortunately, opportunities for customer satisfaction are a dime a dozen. I mean, the less they are satisfied, the more they can be satisfied, right?

And anyway, what are the odds, really, that the Japanese, Germans, and Singaporeans aren't goofing off just as much as us?

Instead of worrying about the hungry nations of the developing world overtaking us, we should be sabotaging their servers by uploading copies of Myst.

THE POST-JOB SOCIETY

You're not a time-waster. You're doing a great job. But do you have one?

The whole idea of the job—full-time, long-term employment, defined wages and benefits and hours—has been in decline since the glory days of IBM in the 60s, the high-water mark of the American standard of living. Cradle-to-grave employment now looks to be a chimera that existed for only a couple of generations of human history.

Indeed, people have had conventional jobs for only a handful of decades, starting somewhere in the early 19th century, peaking in the industrial mid-20th century, and exhibiting definite signs of wear and tear as we draw near the millennium mark. "Jobs" were a side effect of centralized technology—assembly lines, big manufacturing, big government, mainframe computing. As that technological era fades and is replaced by decentralized networked technology—home PCs, wireless, portability—jobs will inevitably fade as well. The long production run ("Head those Mustangs down to the corral!") is a thing of the past; today's manufacturing is increasingly customized, calling for flexible labor, not a permanent, standing workforce.

LEST WE FORGET

During the glory days of PCs, from 1980 to 1985, a thousand brands of desktop models, sporting a wide array of operating systems, popped onto the market. The proliferation of brands came to an end when the IBM Intel standard was finally adopted, and nearly everything was a 100-percent-compatible clone. These are just some of the names that I and associates on Usenet were able to come up with. Can you think of any that are missing?

Acorn, Altair MITS, Altos, Amiga, Amstrad, Apple, Apple Lisa, Apricot, Archimedes, Atari, Atom, Avion, BBC Micro, Billings 104, California Computer Systems, Canon Cat, Cantab Ace, Casu Super C, Challenger OSI, Coleco Adam, Columbia, Commodore Pet, Commodore VIC 20, Commodore 64, 128, Compucolor, Compupro S100, Computhink MiniMax, COSMAC ELF, SuperElf, VIP, Cromemco S100, Darius, DEC Rainbow, DECmate, Delta Gold, Digital DEC PDP-8, Digital Group,

(Continued on page 104)

103

Dragon 32 and 64, Eagle, Electron, Enterprise Elan, Everex, Exidy Sorcerer, FastMicro FastData, Franklin Ace, Future Technology Systems, Gimix SS-50 systems, Grundy Newbrain, Heathkit, Hewlett-Packard HP PCs, HH Tiger, Hyperion, Hyundai, IMSAI, Intecolor, InterSystems, Intertec Superbrain, Ithaca Audio, Jupiter Wavemate, Kaypro, Kentucky Fried Computer, KIM 1, Micro Works SS-50, Microtan, Mindset, Morrow Designs Thinker Toys, Morrow Decision, MSI Systems 6800, Nanocomp, Netronics, North Star, Northgate, Northstar Horizon, Ohio Scientific, Olympus, Oric, Oric Atmos, Osborne 1, Otrona Attaché, Panasonic Executive Partner, Peach I, Percom, PERQ, PolyMorphic Systems Poly 88, Processor Technologies SOL, RCA, Research Nimbus, Rockwell AIM, Seequa Chameleon, Sharp MZ and PC, Sinclair Spectrum, Smoke Signal Broadcasting, Sony MSX, Sord M5, South Western Technical Products, Sperry PC, Sphere 6800, Tandon, Tangerine, TANO Outpost II, Tatung, Tatung Einstein, Technico 9900, Tecmar, Televideo, Texas Instruments TI Pro, TI-99, Toshiba MSX, TRS-80 UK101 Softy1, Softy2, Victor Sirius 1 (seriously!), Wang, Wyse, Xerox Model 3000, Yamaha MSX, Zenith

Our dads had jobs. We may or may not have jobs. Chances are, we have already given up jobs to become entrepreneurs, consultants, or freelancers. Or we share a job with another person. Or we are just plain unemployed.

"A century from now," William Bridges wrote in a recent article in *Fortune*, "Americans will look back and marvel that we couldn't see more clearly what was happening. They will remark how fixated we were on this game of musical jobs in which, month after month, new waves of people had to drop out. They will sympathize with the suffering we were going through but will comment that it came from trying to play the game by the old rules."[3]

Technology is a driving reason for this decline, and it works on both ends. Higher productivity per person is made possible by word processors over typewriters, robots over assemblers, expert systems over flesh-and-blood experts. Thanks to augmentation, organizations need far fewer people to do much more work.

On the worker side, PCs are tempting many of the more enterprising of us to shuck off the chains of employment and try our luck on our own. In an organization we are limited by our function—we are accountants, sales people, store managers. On our own we can be whatever we want to be, crossing every functional line.

The result is that we are evolving into a nation, or at least a subclass, of consultants.

It's been gathering steam a while. A *New Yorker* cartoon ten years ago showed a cross-section of an ant colony and clearly labeled the players there—the queen, the drone, the worker, and carrying a little ant briefcase, the consultant (consult-ant?).

The image is ludicrous because we expect ants to have powerful feelings of community and ownership. If some rotten kid scuffs the top of an anthill with a galosh, you can bet a dollar that the regular ants will suspend their usual functions and chip in to repair the smooshed roof.

But the consulting ant? How strongly does he relate to the anthill? Chances are he does not even live there any more but has set up private digs in an enterprise office suite out along the beltway.

As the technological trend against jobs continues, more and more people will get sucked into the ranks of the alternatively employed—leased employees, telecommuters, free agents, executives on loan, consultants, temps, and other nontraditionals. The huge sucking sound may be coming from our own workplaces—it is the sound of hourly employees being blown through the corporate revolving doors. To put it bluntly, dependent employees are being replaced by independent contractors—by the busload. Even people with jobs are moving from situation to situation more frequently than before. *Lifelong employment* is a phrase seldom heard any more; replacing it is the idea of the *multiple career*—people stepping from profession to profession as technologies and markets emerge, mature, and wither rapidly away.

> "I submit to the people a small invention by my invention, by means of which you alone may, without any effort, perform all the operations of arithmetic, and may be relieved of the work which often times fatigues your spirit."
>
> *Blaise Pascal*[4]

This doubtless means many good things. It means a lot of tubby corporations are admiring their svelte new figures in the mirror. Though we employees think we are all precious and as unique as snowflakes in the eye of God, to the bottom line we are just ballast. Flex employment is a solid winner for employers.

And it's terrific for hourly workers with solid skills, a decent comfort level with technology, and an entrepreneurial bent. They can go from making $20 to $100 per hour overnight—enough to keep the dental plan.

But what about everyone else—how do Riley, Bunker, and Bundy fit into the postjob society? Their skills are middling at best, and narrow. Their educations, so-so. On average, most people are average. Twenty percent of today's high school students never graduate. Face it, we're just not equipped for the go-go world of consultancy. How does a freelance waitperson catch on in such a world, or the independent muffler repairman, or plastics extruder, or consulting nurse?

Finley's Fifth Paradox cuts with a vengeance: *The technology-rich get richer, and the rest get buried.* There is a bright future out there for the swift, the educable, and the aggressive, one-person companies that can identify and exploit profitable niches, with themselves and the knowledge they have amassed as their product. That top tier can be very large—perhaps 50 million Americans or more.

> "Computers make it easier to do a lot of things, but most of the things they make it easier to do don't need to be done."
>
> *Andy Rooney*[5]

But the rest of us, unless we change our very natures, are likely to be second-class in every way. Indistinguishable from our third-world counterparts, unwanted cogs for obsolete machines. That's the future that our politicians avoid mentioning in the biennial sweepstakes to shape the future.

What can you to do succeed in the jobless society? Assess your weaknesses. Identify your reluctance. Get skills and encourage everyone else to get them, too.

The post-job employee will be a self-starter, a learner, someone who understands quality and makes it the basis of the working relationship.

The post-job workplace will not operate on the basis of eight-hour shifts. Indeed, it may not be a "place" at all. Work processes will be a moveable feast, with technology connecting disparate locations and time zones.

Which prompts the glummest assessment of all: If the skills market is opened up beyond the conventional limits of time and location, what assurance is there that the worker of the future will be American?

Our fabled superior productivity to the contrary notwithstanding, there is none.

The Augmented Entrepreneur

One of the most cherished myths of personal computing is that, in the brave new world of the electronic cottage, a single person can replace a skyscraperful of support staff and lateral functions. Our hypothetical, augmented accountant Pat appeared to replace a Big 6 accounting firm single-handedly.

With a word processor, you can take charge of your communications. With a spreadsheet, you become your own finance manager. With a database, you become your own inventory chief/marketing whiz. With desktop publishing, you can be your own ad and art department.

Having a PC in the office is the best possible way to make yourself independent. This is the unspoken subtext of just about every book, article, and advertisement in the computer world. To heck with big balky business structures; you can do it all better, faster, and cheaper with new, improved IBM with Sexium.

Well, it's not quite true. Yes, you can do and/or be all these things. But will you be any good at any of them? There is an old adage, invented back when cottage industry meant something much humbler, that flies in the face of the ethic of the electronic cottager—*Stick to your knitting.*

Working in a regular office, the average person is a specialist. He or she may be a claims adjuster or a researcher or a technician or a line manager. He has a posted job description listing six or seven required skills and specifying three or four job tasks. Technically (though this is more frowned on by the day), any task falling outside the bounds of that written job description can be ignored.

It's not that way when you are on your own. The electronic cottager wears a kazillion hats. He or she is president, paymaster, go-fer, plumber, marketer, communicator, gal/guy Friday, personnel person, project manager, project implementer—the works.

Sure, if you are making a lot of money, you can outsource a lot of these tasks—hire a typist, answering service, transcriber, tax consultant, etc. But, in fact, the more we do ourselves, the more "in charge" we feel we are and the more of our income we get to keep. So we set out to become a one-man band, playing every instrument simultaneously.

And run smack into serious issues of utilization and efficiency. At a central office, ten people may use a laser printer, a FAX, a desktop publishing program, spreadsheet, word processor, all that stuff. In a one-person office, one person alone must make all these things economical.

Invite in an efficiency consultant. He or she will look at all your stuff, see it as the "means to production," the machinery that creates your income, and then ask you to describe how much each one is used. Does your copier copy 500 pages a day? Does your FAX send/transmit 100 copies a day? How many shifts does your "factory" work? If a tool costs $2,500 and that is depreciated in three years, how much revenue does it generate in that time? At what point does your production start to pay for all these toys?

> "The old strategies still focus on the circulation of money rather than knowledge. Yet it is no longer possible to reduce joblessness simply by increasing the number of jobs, because the problem is no longer merely numbers. Unemployment has gone from quantitative to qualitative."
>
> *Alvin Toffler*[6]

Finally, there is the matter of the obsolescence curve in technology. If you buy a piece of equipment or a software program, you had better put it to work that very day and start recouping your expenses, because time flies on the techno planet—one morning you will wake up and that program you never learned will be passé.

Bottom line: You can't afford to let all this expensive equipment sit idle.

Most of us don't worry about these issues. We figure, what the heck, we have $2,000 burning a hole in our checkbook—why not splurge and buy a page scanner? The fact that clients may require us to scan a total of twenty pages per year does not daunt us. The capability, we tell ourselves—we have the capability. We have our bases covered. It is a competitive edge: doggone it, we won't lose business because we didn't have a page scanner.

The thesis here is that effective self-management requires that the independent contractor make some very hard and very serious decisions about what he/she is good at and should stick with, and what he/she is lousy at and should get someone else to do.

The issue of knowledge and human limitations crops up. If we have a hard disk with 20 full-size programs like WordPerfect, PowerPoint, CorelDraw, etc., on it, that is a lot to learn and a lot to remember.

Most of us achieve, in short order, a level of intuitive familiarity with our word processor, spreadsheet, and perhaps our business database. These are the top-tier, use-em-everyday programs. The second tier, however, is harder to remember, because we do not use these programs as often—desktop publishing, money management, time billing, graphics. Then we have a third tier that, because we never get beyond the dabbling stage, we never quite learn, and thus never can capitalize on.

It's that third tier that kills us. To put it simply, we can't do everything, and if we can't do everything, we can't afford everything. And even if we can afford everything, it still makes no sense to buy things we can't realistically use. Acquiring all this stuff, fun as it is, distracts us from work that we need to do, money that might be made, and our acquiring greater mastery of those tools that are critical to our business missions.

Technology can set us free, or it can make fools of us. Don't let it define your business tasks. That's what customers are for. Stick to your knitting, or your knitting will stick to you.

> "Once a new technology rolls over you, if you're not part of the steamroller, you're part of the road."
>
> *Stewart Brand*[7]

What Industry Must Do

If companies tear up their old contract with employees and the implied promise of security, they should create a new contract that spells out the new responsibilities. Either people are as disposable as Dixie cups or they are not. Companies can't mutter new-age nostrums about empowerment and quality one minute and pass out poisoned Kool-Aid the next.

Remember that with globalization comes knowledge. The whole world is watching your corporate behavior. Behave responsibly as if you think it's right—no one will hold it against you.

What You Must Do

Get skills and encourage everyone else to get them, too. Plan on spending eight weeks every year in school learning something new.

"A Computerworld study conducted in the late 1980s concluded that fewer than half of America's top executives were using computers. In other words, the people most responsible for making the ultimate decisions about computers in most companies were least equipped to do so."

James Krobe, Jr.[8]

Assess your weaknesses. Contract employees survive by covering all their bases. This means identifying your reluctances and working to overcome them. The power user, for example, should bolster his people skills. The worrier should realize that the great danger isn't a system crash but a career crash.

Be less generic. Pluggers, take note. You are less likely to be a replaceable cog if you can boast unique skill combinations.

Be a utility player. Guys who can play every infield position ride the bench most days in baseball, but they command high salaries because they are versatile. No rule says a machinist can't learn the rudiments of spreadsheet finance or an engineer can't master general office software.

Be a self-starter, a learner, someone who understands quality and makes it the basis of the working relationship. In an unsupervised future, the winners will be those who don't need supervision. The dreamer who dreams the right dream can own the world.

CHAPTER ■ 6

Technology Without Bankruptcy

The Challenge of Affordable Computing

In which is explored the nettlesome problem of machines costing money, and the pain that comes of running out of same, plus thoughts on using technology in one's investments, and why that is a poor idea

e talk a lot about productivity as the end-all driver behind our work technologies, but let's not kid ourselves. The real driver is money, profits, and material advantage. We all want more, and computers look to many of us like a good way to get more.

The problem is, it is by no means certain that computers guarantee anyone material success. As we discussed in Chapter 3, computers have helped increase productivity, but they haven't exactly been our economic salvation. In bottom-line terms—this is a gross generalization, but pretty much true—they seem to cost about as much as they save.

This doesn't prevent people from holding out great hopes for the enriching power of PCs. House Speaker Newt Gingrich drew fire with his suggestion that one way to eliminate welfare would be to give every welfare recipient in the country a laptop computer. With a handhold on the information age, poor people will be able to master skills, win jobs, explore cyberspace, and start enterprises of their own.

The idea lasted all of about 47 seconds in the public mind and was immediately shot down. (Just think about the inevitable bidding war between IBM and the clonemakers to sell the government 10 million laptops costing $2,000 each.) But it illustrated a truth about the great era of technology that even conservative politicians concede:

DESTITUTION
Paradox #6

You can't afford it; you can't afford to be without it.

empowerment costs money, quite a lot of it in fact, and not everyone can afford to step to the front of the line and get empowered.

American corporations know technology costs money. AT&T, both a user and creator of technology, spent $4.2 billion on information systems in 1994. A firm with 10,000 professional positions must foot the bill for approximately 10,000 PCs. Even if that company is a bottom-feeder and buys only last year's models from second-tier companies, the annual bill per workstation looks something like this:

bare-bones PC	$ 600	($1,800 PC over 3 years life)
faxmodem	40	($80 over 2 years)
CD-ROM and soundcard	150	($450 over 3 years)
extra memory	200	(every year the standard rises)
CompuServe, Internet	300	subscription and fees per year
networked printer	250	($2,500 printer shared by 5 stations to last 2 years)
shared scanner	100	($1,000 scanner shared by 5 stations to last 2 years)
shared copier	75	($3,000 copier shared by 20 workers to last 2 years)
software	2,000	(per year)
telephone	2,400	total costs per year
supplies	1,000	paper, toner, staples, etc.
repairs	500	a guess
training, tech support	150	manuals, videos, fee-based support
miscellaneous stuff	250	
Total IS investment per worker annually	$7,865	

This is not an outlandish estimate; lots of nonspecialized companies spend twice this amount annually per employee. When you consider the world's average annual adult income is about $2,500, you know a central truth of the golden age of technology: it ain't for everyone.

If you're the employee on whom this technology is lavished, you take this up-front investment for granted. Of course you have all that stuff—you need it to do your work. But for everyone else the sheer cost of buying and maintaining office technology is a back-breaker.

WHAT CAN YOU DO TO MAKE TECHNOLOGY MORE AFFORDABLE: FINANCIAL QUESTIONNAIRE

Answer True or False

1. _____ I pay for my own equipment and software.

2. _____ My employers see technology as a cost, not as an investment.

3. _____ I take no tax deductions from my technology purchases.

4. _____ I usually have to borrow to buy, or put purchases on my credit card.

5. _____ When I buy, cost plays an important part in deciding what I get.

6. _____ Sometimes I save up until I have the cash to buy what I need.

7. _____ I sometimes shop for used equipment, liquidated models, and old versions of software, to save money.

> "I don't like money actually, but it quiets my nerves."
>
> *Joe Louis*[1]

8. _____ In my business, what I do on my PC is not my company's end-product (examples: accounting, publishing, CAD), but a support function.

9. _____ I have no way to show how technology increases my productivity or value to my organization.

10. _____ I would love to see, just once, how much better I could work with top-quality equipment and software.

If you answered TRUE to five or more of these questions, welcome to the club. You are grounded in economic reality, and you have to be careful with your dollars. If you answered FALSE to five or more, congratulations. Yours are the circumstances the rest of us aspire to.

KEYBOARD ODDITIES

You don't have to open up the back of your PC to find mysteries. There are scads of them staring you right in the face every day, from your computer keyboard.

Sure, you get the gist of the regular QWERTY keys. They are mostly self-explanatory. But there are keys there that were never on regular typewriters. And there are keys you thought you understood, like # and @, that have stories behind them.

Function keys. F1, F2, F3, etc. Function keys were developed back in the mainframe era. They were developed by some unknown genius with one foot in the world of software and one in the world of hardware. He felt there were not enough regular keys to perform all the tasks required by existing software. The function keys were assignable by nature: each one could be programmed to perform a different task, like a macro. They were a boon to techies because they saved data re-entry time. On desktop computers, they first appeared on the Commodore VIC-20, then on the IBM PC.

(Continued on page 115)

HIGH TECH ON A LOW BUDGET

Some of us are eagles. We situate ourselves high in the sky, so that at the first instant of technological innovation—Windows 95, DOS 6.0, or the latest Hewlett-Packard LaserJet—we may swoop down and have our way with it.

Being an eagle is expensive.

Others of us are bottom-fishers. We troll the floor of the pond, feeling in the murk for the junk no one else wants or the market failed to embrace. If the price is attractive, we haul in our line.

You'll find bottom-fishers in a number of places. We are the people hanging around liquidation centers and used electronic equipment stores, holding cable-ends up to the fluorescent lights, wondering if we can hook this old teletype machine up to our kid's Apple II+. We are the people who buy our electronics at Saturday morning tag sales.

But more than that, we are the people who buy obsolete, refurbished, and odd-lot merchandise through mail order companies like DAK (800-325-0800), Damart (800-729-9000), and Surplus Software (800-753-7877). We prowl the pages of Computer Shopper, looking for a mail merchant that can cut another $10 off an upgrade we have been dying for.

Get on one mailing list, soon you're on a dozen. The main caution is, customer support for bottom-fishers is nil. Do not expect upgrade notices from manufacturers, many of whom have skipped whatever country they were operating in and are now, officially, God knows where. Buy a software product and look in vain for a warranty card or tech support number. It has been discontinued, and that fancy stuff isn't for the likes of you. You're a bottom-fisher.

But call, buy, assemble, enjoy. You are on your own. And if it ends up in a box on your closet floor, so what? You got a great deal.

LET US PRAISE THE BLEEDING EDGE

Back to the eagles. Those of us dwelling in the main part of the forest envy these creatures, flying high over the canopy, up in the mountains, buying the items they want, the day they want it, always in style. But we should be grateful to them. Eagles pay a frightful price for fashion. While we search for a good notebook computer in the $2,000 range, they are plunking down $4,500 for a state of the art Toshiba, with wireless modem.

Why do they do it? To show off, probably. But more than that, they love new things, and the price tag does not scare them away, as it does us.

They were a staple of early programs like WordStar, WordPerfect and dBase2. But average everyday users never warmed to them, so when Microsoft created Windows and its mouse-driven interface, they made a concerted effort not to go "Function-key crazy." A full-size 103-key keyboard with function keys at the left side is one long slab of plastic. Their diminished use made it possible to put function keys atop the keyboard, rather than at the side—an absolute necessity for laptops.

ALT , CTRL, and SHIFT. Like function keys, ALT and CTRL were developed to create more keyboard options. But whereas function keys are programmable—they can do whatever the user tells them to do—ALT and CTRL send fixed signals to the processor. Every character you type consists of eight bits, which we will call bit 7 through bit 0, with 7 being the most significant, and 0 being the least significant. The six least significant bits (5-0) were adequate to handle the uppercase letters, the numbers, and some special

(Continued on page 116)

symbols. On a typewriter, the SHIFT key lifted the key chassis so the lower level of each key, carrying the upper case letters, struck the ribbon. On a PC the SHIFT key sets bit 6 high, turning the lower case letters into upper case, and changing the special symbols. The CTRL key forces both bits 6 and 5 low, accessing the control codes. Through this all, bit 7 has been low. The ALT key forces bit 7 high, so yet another set of 128 character codes becomes available.

Slashes. We are familiar with the forward slash (/), also called the stroke. The forward slash (which is the most common used form for division) appeared on manual typewriters. But the first real use of them was in early computers, which substituted the forward slash for the division sign. The backslash (\) was added in the 1970s to perform mathematical computations. We use it today to indicate subdirectories.

SysRq. This is a throwback to the IBM 3270 terminals (which your PC can pretend to be, though I'll bet you it has never needed to). You hit this key when you wanted to get the mainframe's attention: System Request.

(Continued on page 117)

Their willingness to lay out cash for new products helps the rest of us immeasurably, even the bottom-feeders lurking at the bottom of the pond. These people bought the Lisa, for $10,000, way back in 1984. Not many of them bought a Lisa, but enough did that Apple saw the market possibilities of a PC that met users halfway.

Then this same bleeding edge shelled out $2,495 for the first Macintosh computers, despite terrible storage and memory limitations. They bought up the early gas plasma laptop screens, which went on to become a significant feature in lower-end machines. They bought the first home computers, the first CD ROMs, the first, and very expensive, sound cards. They bought the first 28.8 kbps modems. They will be the first people to install ISDN phone lines, to permit the massive, rapid data downloads to enable Mosaic to fly on the World Wide Web.

Without these people willing to throw their money down the well, none of these trends would have worked their way down the slope of technology where the rest of us were crouching.

There is a not-very-nice tendency in our country to mock losers, even (especially) losers with great talent or ambition, that fall just short of the mark. The PC world seems especially cruel this way, and I don't know why. Questers and dreamers know what I'm talking about.

It makes more sense to celebrate the also-rans and almost-weres, the entrepreneurs who throw themselves at new ideas, and to encourage entrepreneurial consumers to keep spending their money on new ventures.

Computer technology has a way of commoditizing itself very rapidly. You can nearly always buy the fastest speed of modem for about $150. But without our eagles, products would never get the chance in the market to depreciate so that we could afford it. The plain vanilla clone systems on our desks needed those first costly Lisas and the IBM ATs to create demand.

Right now, a raft of next-generation technologies is almost ready to drop down to Main Street price levels—voice processing, thumbprint security, optical character recognition, and digital telephony.

If you want the new technologies to drift down to the bottom, don't make fun of the people testing them up top.

CAN YOU GET RICH USING TECHNOLOGY?

I don't do a lot of name-dropping, but I happen to have spent a year in

Break. This key interrupts any program running in BASIC. Again, chances are you've never needed to do this.

@ Everyone knows what this is, but no one is sure what to call it. We call it the "at-sign" because it means "at" or "costing," as in "15 bu @ 7/6 ea." It's remarkable that we haven't devised a better name for it than at-sign. I asked Internet users around the world what they call it in their languages. Germans call it *Klammeraffe*. Norwegians have four names for it: *kr°llalfa* (curled alpha), *grisehale* (pig's tail), *nabla* and *at-tegn* (at-sign). Swedes call it *kanelbulle* (cinnamon bun). Danes call it *snable* a (trunk a). The French call it, variously, *a commercial, a enroule* (rolled a), and *arrobas* or *arrobasque*, which resembles the Chilean *arroa*. Russians also call it *commercial a.*

Other spoken names for keyboard characters:

~ tilde, twiddle

! bang, pling, shriek

hash, pound, mesh, scratch, sharp, octothorpe, *skigard* (Norwegian) (also the Chinese character for communal farm)

(Continued on page 118)

my professional life with one of the handful of people in the world who went on to become genuine technology multimillionaires.

He's Paul Brainerd, founder of Aldus Technology, maker of PageMaker. PageMaker, the world's first desktop publishing program, was designed in 1984 to achieve, at low cost and on an easy to use, what-you-see-is-what-you-get basis, what commercial page layout systems were costing $50,000 to do. It was a smash sensation, and it gave the fledgling Macintosh computer what it had been dying for—a "killer app," an application that, once explained to people, they could not live without. PageMaker did for the Mac what Lotus 1-2-3 had done for the IBM PC two years before.

I'm sure Paul wouldn't remember me from Adam, but we worked together in 1971 on the staff of the *Minnesota Daily*, the school paper at the University of Minnesota in Minneapolis. I was illegally reviewing books for the paper under a dozen pseudonyms, so as to earn more than the allowable weekly salary. Paul was editor, and he had no idea of my Sybil disobedience.

$ cash, dollar, string

% cent, percent

^ caret, up, hat

& and, ampersand (in Danish, *Anders And*, the name there for Donald Duck)

¦ pipe

* splat, star, splotch, butthole

( ) open close, parenthesis, parens

< > brackets

{ } open and close curly

/ slash

\ slosh

. dot, point

- dit

; semi

: colon

The most intriguing key names I have come across are:

The Yu-Shiang Whole Fish, a key that appeared on early Lisp machine.

The Cokebottle, any key you needed but wasn't on your keyboard.

I was a techno ignoramus, hammering out my life's work on a Hermes 3000 portable steel typewriter but doing my best to pass myself off as a reporter—soft Fedora, press pass in the hatband, etc. This was in the basement of the journalism school and I did not want people to suspect I was anything but a journalist.

I remember loving Fridays, when we would put together the following Monday's special section. We rolled up our sleeves and pulled type galleys from a photocomposition unit. Newspaper type was a photo that you scissored and pasted into place on a dummy page.

But Paul seemed oblivious to that requirement. He was tall, good-natured, very smart, a little quiet—the exact opposite of most editors. My memory of him was that he was always walking through the newsroom, measuring walls, counting electrical outlets. What sort of journalist carried a flathead screwdriver in his back pocket at all times? He acted more like a building super than an editor.

But today I understand. Paul was looking for ways to move the newspaper into the future. He was measuring work spaces, studying how people worked, when things happened and when things didn't. His reporters and subeditors ran the day-to-day affairs of the paper. After leaving the paper he tried his hand in straight publishing, but he quickly became entranced by another odd vision—creating software to do page layouts. I don't think he knew a single thing about computers when we worked together. Eleven years later, he was on his way to a fortune as one of the silicon world's first great millionaires. The most recent Computer Industry Almanac pegs his stock holdings at $88 million.[3]

TECHNO BILLIONAIRES	
Stock holdings, year-end 1993[2]	
Bill Gates, Microsoft	$7.01 billion
Paul Allen, Microsoft	$2.73
David Packard, Hewlett-Packard	$1.9
William Hewlett, Hewlett-Packard	$1.51
Gordon Moore, Intel	$1.4
Steven Ballmer, Microsoft	$1.38

Wouldn't it be great if every one of us could carry a screwdriver around in our hip pockets, identify unmet needs, turn the crank, and fill our hats with gold? I probably don't grasp the economics or physics of techno entrepreneurism, but it seems to me that an all-millionaire world would be a happy world.

Well, that's not going to happen. Realistically, there are just four ways we can use PC technology to enrich ourselves. We can:

- use technology to create conventional products and services (entrepreneuring)
- use technology to support business tasks (bookkeeping, correspondence, advertising, etc.)
- use technology to help us put our money to use (investing)

1833. Ada Lovelace meets Charles Babbage. The first software programmer was the daughter of poet Lord Byron, and an assistant to Babbage—Ada Augusta Byron, later known as the Countess of Lovelace. When Babbage died, the countess kept his ideas in the public eye. A century after her death a computer language would be named after her, Ada.

1847. The creation of Boolean logic. People count on fingers and toes, but machines count faster using a simpler mathematics, called binary mathematics, involving 0s and 1s. Philosopher and mathematician George Boole (1815-1864) took binary mathematics a step further in 1847 when he devised a set of algebraic functions relying not on numerical but logical values. Boolean algebra plus binary math provided computers with the core language they would need to work.

(Continued on page 121)

The first is a crapshoot; you could end up either rich like Paul Brainerd or like that fellow you see picking up cans down by the river. The second is a productivity play. The third is a preoccupation of many computer users. It may include tracking investments using spreadsheet or investment programs like Quicken; downloading information about companies from databases like CompuServe and Dow Jones Information Service; buying and selling using on-line vendors; sharing tips and ideas with other investors in on-line forums; and so forth.

The problem is that unless you are already rich, the costs of maintaining all these investment initiatives will prevent you from becoming rich. Look in the back pages of *Money* or *Kiplingers*, or in any general-interest computing magazine. There are software products to help you keep track of investments, monitor market trends, project what-if scenarios, and perform various feats of technical analysis. There are regularly updated disk-based and CD-ROM products telling you everything you want to know about mutual funds, stocks on major exchanges, international currencies, futures, penny stocks, precious metals, even collectibles. There are on-line services that provide real-time price fluctuations, downloadable shareware products, and forums in which you can while away hours conversing on each day's ticker truths.

There is no limit to the number of things you can do to improve your ability to forecast, buy, monitor, and evaluate your investments. And each one costs you money.

Take CompuServe. Please. It is a treasure trove of information about sticker prices, mutual fund trends, information about companies and management. You can download software from it. You can meet in financial forums and conferences and pick experts' brains.

> 1890. **The punch-card machine.** A disciple of Charles Babbage, Herman Hollerith gets short shrift in computer history, but his punch-card tabulator set into motion a flurry of crucial innovations. Developed to help tabulate census figures in 1890, the Hollerith machine sensed punched holes in cards by means of static electricity. In 1911 his Tabulating Machine Company became a cash cow division for a company that would someday be called IBM. Holleriths continued to do office tabulating work into the 1950s.

"You only have to do a very few things right in your life so long as you don't do too many things wrong."

Warren Buffett[4]

And you will go broke trying to make a buck. Subscribing to basic services is only $9.95 per month. But many of the extended services cost upwards of $22.80 per hour (at 14.4 baud). Database fees are even worse; I have rung up fees of $200 in less than an hour of hunting, only to be horrified when my CompuServe bill arrived at month's end.

Now, if you are an investor, you are under a solemn obligation to keep your investment expenses low. You will pick one mutual fund over another because it will charge you $5 less per year in fees. People with millions invested take pains to mail in their annual fees separately, so the $10 is deductible. Shareholders join proxy revolts when expenses rise a fraction of a percent.

So $22.80 per hour is an ostrobogulous amount to add to the cost of investing. Have a care, would-be rich people—the less you use CompuServe, the richer you will be. At least, that has been my experience.

And CompuServe is just one on-line source for financial information. There's also Dow Jones, America Online, Delphi,

"If you do buy a computer, don't turn it on."

Richards' 2nd Law of Data Security[5]

eWORLD, GEnie, Prodigy, plus the entire Internet, with its Usenet newsgroups, FTP addresses, gophers, and World Wide Web sites. That's a lot of geography, and you are not likely to have access to more than one or two of the services. If you are on GEnie, all the information in the world about America Online is of little use to you.

Second, on-line information is of widely varying quality. The expensive stuff, on the big commercial services, tends to be very good. The free stuff, available on the Internet and World Wide Web, is often either incomplete, messy as all get-out, or tainted:

- **Incomplete.** Yes, you can read the current issue of *The Economist* by Internet gopher. But not last week's issue, because the magazine is only offered to lure you into subscribing. It is a showcase, not a database.
- **Messy.** The world's smartest people meet to discuss financial issues in Usenet forums. Also, the world's biggest boneheads. Are you sure you can tell which is which?
- **Tainted.** The net is not the public library. It is seldom the kind of objective, complete information you set out to find. Whatever data is available is only available because someone had a reason for putting it there. Think about that.

There is a bottom line, and it is what it has always been: let the buyer beware.

GETTING RICH BY STEALING

Which leaves one other way to use your PC to enrich yourself —through crime. Where yesterday's money was coins and bills, today's money is nearly imaginary. Credit cards, ATMs, wire transfers, and banking by phone have combined to make finance a technological subspecialty.

Every year, billions of dollars are moved from where they belong to where they shouldn't be, by clever people who have leveraged technology to get rich the really quick way.

There have been cases of people taking as much as $350,000 from a single automated teller machine in a single day. The big investment

> **Hanlon's Razor**—"Never attribute to malice what can be adequately explained by stupidity." Said during times of stress.
>
> **jogging the memory**—An advance in computing in the ABC—Atanasoff-Berry Computer, c. 1938, that enabled computers to continually be reminded of their own memory.
>
> **kludge**—That which functions but only poorly.

house scandals of the 1980s, involving Marty Siegel, Dennis Levine, and Ivan Boesky, were computer crimes, involving illegal access to electronic documents, violation of information "firewalls," and surreptitious moving of funds.

No one can put a number on the amount that embezzlers within companies slide from Column A to Column B every year, because the people committing these crimes are usually the people in charge of preventing such crimes. Since the money exists in only a virtual way, as electrons in the wiring and pixels on the screen, people do not get as upset.[6]

Although every major police force now has a white collar crime task force, there isn't a great deal of political pressure to crack down on this class of criminal. It is neither violent nor public. Yet it is one of the primary causes of inflation and higher insurance rates (and federal bailout dollars), which should be a concern of all of ours.

> "Money has moved from the tactile to one of the most abstract realms we inhabit, which is mathematics."
>
> *Joel Kurtzman*[7]

What You Can Do

Rely only on yourself. You have been alive long enough to know that one reason the world exists is to put daylight between you and your money. Spending money to make money should be kept to a minimum.

Know yourself. Techno enthusiasts can be their own worst enemies. Just as you have attitudes about technology (worrier, dreamer, plugger, etc.), you have attitudes about money. Only you know what rationalizations you are likely to make—which corners you are likely to cut and which you are likely to paint yourself into.

"Save a little money each month and at the end of the year you'll be surprised at how little you have."

Ernest Haskins[8]

Buy systems by their annual operating costs, not just their sticker price. A knock-off clone is no bargain if its components are the cheapest on the planet and need frequent replacing. A system that is down as often as it is up is not much of a system at all. Read the annual reliability reports in *PC Magazine*.

Set up a savings plan with a money market mutual fund, automatically setting aside $100 a month. This way you always have some money set aside—for purchases, upgrades, or repairs.

Be a bottom-fisher. For generic requirements, buy low. (Pay high for mission-critical tools or for tools unique to your business or work.) Shop liquidation centers. Discount catalogs. Swap meets. Check out BBS rooms where people are unloading or trading older equipment.

Borrow wisely. It may be better to borrow money today to buy technology than to wait, because while you save you will be losing ground to your competition. But be careful that you are not buying out of impulse, an easy thing to do. Never borrow because you want something. Dreamers are asked to read that sentence until it sinks in. Only buy on credit when the thing you are purchasing will pay for itself. Know your repayment habits. If you stretch payments out too far, the cost rises exponentially.

Look for credit freebies. Superper hour stores and direct merchandisers often feature interest-free periods. Don't buy from this source in order to take advantage of this credit. And by all means pay the entire balance off before the meter starts ticking again—finance companies more than compensate for their free-interest periods with sky-high interest periods later. But if you have already decided to buy from a superstore, look into their credit "sales."

"I never buy at the bottom, and I always sell too soon."

Nathan Rothschild[9]

Create redundant systems. If you have the money, consider setting up the equivalent of a backup system. If you run a Pentium, hold on to last year's 486. Set it up so that the tape drive in the new computer can slide into the old one at a moment's notice. Buy identical keyboards for both machines, so that your hands don't have to learn a new language when one system goes down.

Buy according to your needs. When buying a system or major component, you can buy from a local retail store, a mail order store, or a computer manufacturer. Each approach generally offers several advantages:

■ **Local store.** Unless you are a computer whiz, buying a computer can be an intimidating experience. Knowing a good local store to go to, where the sales people have a reputation for "taking care of their customers," can make a tough decision a lot easier. With a local store, you have a living, breathing salesman to deal with. You can haggle about a system's price. If something goes wrong, later, you don't have to bundle up your computer in its original case, pay the shipping to some repair depot hundreds of miles away, and face being computerless for weeks at a time. Best of all, retail stores offer instant gratification. Get in your car, drive to the mall, plunk down your cash, cart your machine home, and boot it up—all in one day.

> **TOP TEN SIGNS YOU BOUGHT A BAD COMPUTER**
>
> 10. Lower corner of screen has the words "Etch-A-Sketch" on it.
> 9. Its celebrity spokesman is that "Hey Vern!" guy.
> 8. In order to start it you need some jumper cables and a friend's car.
> 7. It's slogan is "Pentium: redefining mathematics."
> 6. The "quick reference" manual is 120 pages long.
> 5. Whenever you turn it on, all the dogs in your neighborhood start howling.
> 4. The screen often displays the message "Ain't it break time yet?"
> 3. The manual contains only one sentence: "Good Luck!"
> 2. The only chip inside is a Dorito.
> 1. You've decided that your computer is an excellent addition to your fabulous paperweight collection.[10]

Hiring and training a thousand people in a dozen different markets, on the other hand, is a nightmare. Employees need guidance, and they should be empowered; they seldom are. Note the unempowered expressions on the faces of employees at certain local office supply stores. Placing stores in every large city means your retail chain has

> "I have enough money to last me the rest of my life, unless I buy something."
>
> *Jackie Mason*

much higher overhead than a one-location mail house. Someone pays for that overhead—you. Though some superstores are starting to offer system bargains competitive with mail order prices, retail systems generally cost 10–20 percent more than systems bought by mail.

■ **Mail order.** The biggest attractions of mail order stores are price and variety. For years, mail order outfits have thrived by offering adventurous buyers a virtual department store of hardware and software products, at deep discounts, often bypassing state sales taxation. Modern mail order stores do a pretty good job of training their sales people to know their product lines so they can answer your questions. Many people are afraid of mail order, though. Those people on the other end of the phone are strangers in a strange state. You can't "kick the tires" or "test drive" a system by mail.

Of course, you have to wait for the mail. It is not unusual to have to wait 7–10 days to have a system delivered by truck. And, shipping costs can eat away at the money you saved up front.

■ **Factory.** The big advantages of buying direct from the manufacturer are price and configurability. If you buy a Zeos computer by phone, you can have it equipped exactly the way you want it.

> "I went to the bank and went over my savings. I found out I have all the money I'll ever need. If I die tomorrow."
>
> *Henny Youngman*

They sell thousands of machines every month, so they have the best inventories—no ringers, no bait-and-switch, no scratch-and-dents. If you must buy a "lemon" computer, buy it from the factory. They will be eager and able to make you happy again—most stores won't. If you have a problem, you know that the company will know exactly how to solve it; store technical support, by contrast, is spread too thin across too many product lines. And most manufacturers now offer local service contracts, so you can have your system fixed without having to ship it off to who-knows-where for who-knows-how-long.

■ **Your repair partner.** There is one other way to buy. Buy your next PC from the people that have been repairing your current one. Face it, with today's complex systems you need an on-call techie partner to keep you up and running. Will they have the lowest price on a system? Probably not—but they, better than anyone, will know how to upgrade you to new system functionality at half the price—by swapping motherboards and peripherals as your needs evolve and as your pocketbook permits.

"You pay a small deposit," said the salesperson, "and then make no more payments for six months." "Who told you about us?" demanded the prospective customer.

I have bought my last two computers from a repair shop. They advise me on buying decisions, and if anything goes wrong, by God they make it right, and fast—because our relationship is geared for the long haul, beyond the point of purchase.

CHAPTER ■ 7

Can We Survive Computing?

Death and Disease Were Not Supposed to Be Part of the Deal

The dismaying specter of stress injuries, radiation, headaches, eye aches, and spinal problems

hen computers came into our lives, we made several implicit contracts with them.

On the plus side, they would increase our productivity.

On the minus side, they would add misery to our lives in the form of increased amounts of junk mail, annoying new words people could use at parties and make us feel stupid for not knowing, and billing mistakes that, though they ruined our credit records, were not really anybody's fault.

Some would say that's not a very balanced contract, but wait—things get worse. Many people are now saying that computers are ruining, or have already ruined, their physical health. As in shortened life span and deteriorated quality of life.

Here is the list of damages:

Headache, eyestrain, and worse. Staring at a monitor 8, 10, 12 hours a day takes its toll. We've all experienced headache and eyestrain. But claims have been made that computer work can cause permanent damage to the eyes, including myopia and cataracts.

Hand and wrist injuries. Computer users today suffer from the same maladies that typists have suffered from for decades—painful and nearly untreatable repetitive strain injuries like wrist tendinitis and carpal tunnel syndrome.

Spinal problems. Sitting all day in one position, hunched over a keyboard causes stiffness and aggravates existing conditions like arthritis or curvature of the spine.

Radiation-caused illnesses. Reports persist that the rays emitted from your computer monitor can cause birth defects, miscarriages, and stillbirths in pregnant women and leukemia and other cancers in the rest of us.

Those late addenda make a bad deal look stunningly worse. Even the most avid computerophile is not eager to lay down his life for his machine. Productivity increases are no recompense for health problems.

THE TRUTH

But what is the truth to all these claims? Isn't it logical, given the number of people using computers, that they will experience their fair share of disability and disease? Which of these health problems are to be taken seriously? Which ones can be prevented, and how? Which ones are unpreventable and may make you rethink this whole computer thing?

PAIN
Paradox #7

That which does not destroy you can still cause major problems.

---

loop—When a product endlessly repeats a requested task and you have to turn the system off to make it stop.

mantissa—The fractional part of a number expressed in floating-point notation.

nano—The Greek root for dwarf; a prefix meaning one-billionth of something.

plug and play—A state arrived at when your computer configures itself to whatever you want to make it work with. Also, chimera, mirage.

The good news is that there is no smoking-gun evidence that computer users suffer a higher incidence of any kind of cancer than the non-computer-using public. Computers don't get a bill of good health from doctors, and many are calling for more research into computers and cancer. But if there is a computer/cancer link, it is far from obvious.

The bad news is that most everything else in the above list is more or less true. Computers can indeed cause eyestrain and headaches, although there is nothing unique to computers here. Using computers causes the same strain that intensive reading or writing or typing causes. A 1985 study of newspaper people revealed that users of VDT screens had a tendency to become slightly cross-eyed. A Canadian study, however, showed that the vision of computer users didn't deteriorate any faster over five years than the vision of non-computer users.[1]

Should pregnant women avoid computers? A 1988 study showed that women working more than 20 hours a week at a VDT screen had a higher rate of miscarriages. However, the researchers said that may not mean much—women working 20 hours a week were exposed to other factors which could account for the blip—deadlines, working conditions, Clarence Thomas.

There is no proof anywhere that computers cause harm to un-born babies.

VISUAL WORKING CONDITIONS ARE CHANGING RAPIDLY[2]

Time	Economic Evolution	Viewing Distance at Work
pre-1600s	Hunter-Gatherer	Far
1600s–1800s	Farmer	Far
1900s	Laborer	Varied
1960s	Clerk	Near
1980s–1990s	Information Worker	Near

BACK PROBLEMS

Bad posture, bad furniture, and long hours have combined to put a whammy on thousands of office workers. Computer-related back injury has kept a new genera-tion of chiropractors in polyester suits. Sedentary habits related to computing have also been linked to obesity, hemorrhoids, and, indi-rectly, to heart disease and death.

Backaches are a story all by themselves. My pals in the computer repair business lift equipment all the time, and though they are not the type to complain, they have worn little pain lines onto their faces. Computers are heavy and awkward, and lifting them routinely is an open invitation to back problems.

Just sitting in front of them is almost as bad. Sitting at the wrong height, or the wrong distance from the keyboard, or in the wrong kind of chair, can lead, bit by bit and day by day, to chronic lower back strain that can be phenomenally painful.

Solutions are often as problematic as the problems themselves. As an occasional sufferer from back twinges, I have tried some of the radically redesigned "back chairs" on the market, including one that looks like an upholstered swastika. Instead of sitting conventionally, you sort of kneel/sit in it. It does give you a nice, feathery balance when you work. But if you need to rise suddenly to answer the doorbell, you risk tangling your feet and stumbling.

Bottom line: no matter how you sit at the computer, if you sit there all the time, you're going to pay the price. A good practice, apart from having your chair, desk, etc., redesigned by an aerospace engineer, is to get up and do something physical every now and then. The human form was not designed for prolonged sitting.

Ironically, a really comfortable chair ("I feel like I could work for 72 hours straight in this!") might be the worst possible chair for you.

HANDS AND WRISTS

Which brings us to hand and wrist problems. Carpal tunnel syndrome and wrist tendinitis, two specific kinds of repetitive stress injuries computer users are prone to, are serious stuff. People who have it complain that their hands feel like they're asleep, weak, stiff, and sore. Others say it's like you just hit a brick wall with your fist. It can end your career.

FOURTEEN CLINICAL TRUTHS ABOUT REPETITIVE STRESS INJURIES[3]

1. RSI is not just one thing.
2. You don't need to have much repetition to induce it.
3. If you smoke, you always get it worse.
4. If anti-inflammatory medications work, you didn't have a bad case.
5. All the ergonomic workstation modifications in the world won't make a significant difference if you don't correct your posture and start taking care of yourself.
6. If you're under stress, you'll do worse.
7. If you've had it for more than three months and are told it's "just tendinitis," you can be sure it's not tendinitis.

(Continued on page 132)

The carpal tunnel is a passageway in your wrist surrounded by bone and ligament; through it passes a nerve. If you are a marathon typist you put great stress on this fragile bridge, and the tendons there may respond by swelling to protect the passageway, putting the nerve

8. If you're seeing an M.D. who says he or she doesn't know what you have, you've found an honest physician.

9. Splints are fine only if they work.

10. Ice is fine only if it works.

11. Heat is fine as long as you apply it to muscles in spasm.

12. If you're sick of taking pills of one sort or another and they don't work, you're not alone.

13. Addressing just the painful part in therapy and not the entire neck to fingertips is substandard treatment.

14. Insurance companies are uniformly ignorant, or obstructionist, or both, when it comes to treating these problems.

in a Bulgarian headlock. The upshot of this neuropathy—loss of feeling in the hands, decreased hand strength, and crippling pain.

Go to a doctor and he/she won't have a pill to make your carpal tunnel better. The prescribed treatment is a computer user's worst nightmare—rest and relaxation. No key entry of any kind. Cortisone sometimes helps. Some doctors turn you over to a surgeon or physical therapist.

Carpal tunnel is a recent phenomenon—manual typists of the bygone era seem not to have had the problem. Some people speculate this could be because the old funky Remington keyboards were actually more ergonomic in design than the "sprawling console" 103-key keyboards in use today. Even so, computer typists suffer the most from carpal tunnel syndrome—people who type 50 or 60 words a minute, hour after hour.

Want to avoid or slow the effects of a lifetime of typing? Change the way you hold your hands when you type. If you are twisting your wrists to be parallel to the keyboard, stop. Hold your hands naturally, with your wrists as relaxed as when they are at your sides.

Perhaps keyboard design will save us from carpal tunnel problems before we are all bent and crippled. Merely substituting mouses and pens for typing is not the answer—many people claim to feel greater tension with these devices than with keys. Microsoft has recently led the way in creating lower-cost, so-called ergonomic keyboards. The emphasis of them is to put the wrists at a natural, arced angle, by separating the keys into two groups, and providing a generous "front porch" for the palms and wrists to rest on when not busy.

I have been using this keyboard, and I have tried several other designs, some of them very eccentric indeed. Retraining your fingers and hands is a frustrating task, particularly if you are in the early stages of injury already and every mistake must be painfully corrected.

Computer people tend to spend too much time in their head, at the keyboard. If this sudden interest in health and computers has a bright side, it is that we are reminded that we have to stand up every now and then, step outside, and see how the roses are doing.

WHAT ABOUT VOICE RECOGNITION?

Four years ago a friend who was concerned about repetitive strain injury confided his strategy: switch from keyboard input to voice activation. As soon as the technology was there, and affordable, he was going for it.

He's still waiting. There are some great products out there, led by Kursweil Voice, with a vocabulary of 60,000 words. You can use your voice to issue basic instructions to your PC: open applications, delete files, etc.

But even Kurzweil, which has been doing voice activation for 20

1843. The fax machine dates back to this year, during the era of telegraphy, before telephones. In that year Alexander Bain was granted a British patent for facsimile transmission. In 1865 the first commercial fax transmission service was established in Paris.

1904. Invention of the vacuum tube. May not sound like much, but the humble vacuum tube, patented in 1904 by Lee De Forest, changed everything. It provided a stable, reliable way for computers to count. It was a primitive digital device: a tube was either off or it was on—0 or 1. Thus the little bulb could replace the more fragile mechanical switch. The first true computers would rely heavily on thousands of blinking tubes. The tube would eventually give way to the transistor, and the transistor to today's microchip.

1945. The PC is first envisioned. "It consists of a desk, and while it can presumably be operated from a distance, it is primarily the piece of furniture at which the user works. On the top are slanting translucent screens on which material can be projected for convenient read-

(Continued on page 134)

ing. There is a keyboard and sets of buttons and levers. Otherwise it looks like an ordinary desk." (Vannevar Bush, describing what a personal computer might be like one day, in a 1945 issue of *Atlantic.*)

1959. The first integrated circuits, invented independently by Jack Kilby and Robert Noyce to replace vacuum tubes, had only a couple of switches or transistors on them. By 1970 memory chips boasted 1,000 miniature transistors. By 1980, new chips contained as many as 64,000 transistors.chfn65 By 1995, semiconductor companies were making chips with 25 million transistors packed into a half-inch chip. Throughout this period, however, the price for a memory chip—about $10—remained constant.

years and whose basic voice product retails for $1,000, is frustrating to use. Computers do not, after 50 years of dealing with it, understand English, or any other language. PCs simply don't know how the sounds you are making should look on the page.

Here's a classic example of verbal ambiguity that a computer can't be expected to parse:

> *Time flies like an arrow*
> *Fruit flies like a banana*

Here's another: *It's hard to recognize speech.* How does your PC know you're not saying, *It's hard to wreck a nice beach?*

Voice recognition is one of those salvation technologies many of us have been pining for but may never come riding to our rescue. When we ask for voice, we are asking computers to understand the subtleties of human thought and expression. You could have a supercomputer, hooked up to the densest expert systems database and most intuitive artificial intelligence logarithm there is—and it still would not be able to get in synch with our natural inclinations to joke, circumambulate, pun, and be vague.

And without voice recognition, we are right back where we started, with keyboards and achy-breaky wrists.

TAKING CARE OF THE EYES

Four years ago, during the week before Christmas, I bought and installed a new VGA monitor, thus giving me my first color computer ever. I celebrated by going blind.

Really. After a few days of the new monitor I developed excruciating headaches, and my vision went to heck in a handbasket. Thinking I was in a medical emergency, I shelled out a couple hundred bucks for eye examinations and glasses. I remember driving in a Minnesota snowstorm on Christmas eve to get the darn things—blinking in sync with the wipers.

My problem, of course, was the monitor. Though it wasn't defective in any way, it was a cheap monitor, and my eyes were overworking to get used to it. Eventually I adjusted the color downward, to the dull realm of hues most appropriate for a computer writer, and after a few days the headaches subsided—I folded up those glasses and put them away for good (cross fingers).

Truth is, an all-nighter computing is as hard on the eyeballs as a marathon race is on the shins. One physician has described a "computer user syndrome" in which our eyes are constantly shifting from monitor to hardcopy to keyboard, each time at a different angle and at a different depth of field.[63] The result—Repetitive Optical Orthopedic Motion Stress, or ROOMS. Angry eyes, stiff neck, headaches, the works.

> Her secret to longevity?
>
> "Keep breathing."
>
> *Sophie Tucker*[4]

There are numerous exercises you can do during the computing day to keep your eyes from getting overtired. Here are three very simple ones that I do a few times a day. I find they not only relax my eyes and frontal lobes but that they subtly refresh me and make me more open to new ideas and perspectives.

- **Rub the eyes.** It seems to calm the little guys down, and you get the side benefit of a light show on the backs of your eyelids. Obviously, you mustn't overdo this.
- **Close the eyes.** Just close them, and take a dozen slow, gentle breaths. When I do this I talk to my eyes. I thank them for doing all my work for me. This little break in the visual day is their recess.
- **Stretch the face.** This is the posture or asana called The Lion in hatha yoga. You open your mouth as wide as you can, arch your eyebrows as high as you can, stick your tongue out, and roll your eyes in big circles. It looks ridiculous, but after I do this I always feel open-minded and more creative.[5]

Painful Irony

I have several friends who have gone through wrenching ordeals because of computer keyboards. In March 1995, a federal lawsuit filed against Apple Computer and IBM by a woman suffering from repetitive stress injuries was dismissed by a jury in Hastings, Minnesota. The jury's message: users are to blame for injuries they suffer, regardless of product design.

To limit potential liabilities, Microsoft now tags its Natural brand of ergonomic keybards with this message:

DO NOT REMOVE THIS TAG!
WARNING

Continuous use of a keyboard may cause Repetitive Stress Injuries or related injuries. See on-line Help, User's Manual, and bottom of keyboard for instructions on using the Wrist Leveler and for important information to reduce your risk of injury.

There is a profound irony in an ergonomic keyboard resorting to this sort of tobacco-industry cautionary. Computers are sometimes referred to as the instruments of the postindustrial age. This is supposed to be a wonderful thing, because the industrial age is often thought of as brutal and insulting to individual intelligence.

In the theory of scientific management propounded almost a century ago by Frederick Taylor, the worker of the modern (industrial) era could only be trusted to do a single thing, over and over. Turning that hex bolt two and a quarter turns counterclockwise, four times a minute, 240 times an hour, 1,920 times a shift—that was the most a human being was deemed capable of doing, even a supervised one. We were muscle machines, and nothing more.

Along come personal computers, and we have a new language and vision of human potential. We talk about the end of drudgery and about machines freeing people up to do the work of the mind.

But we input data into these wonderful machines the way our grandfathers shoveled coal—unrelentingly. We are still muscle machines, our hands still do the brunt of the physical work. Not surprisingly, the muscle machine breaks down. How weird that this tool, which was supposed to liberate us from the industrial age of employee injury, is creating a whole new generation of postindustrial cripples.

Net wisdom: Don't count on industry to save you from bad posture, bad work habits, and a helpless-me attitude. It's your body, it's your computer, and it's your responsibility.

SELECTING AN ERGONOMIST

Humanity has advanced to such a high state in recent years that even the Bushmen of southern Africa must be familiar with the phrase "ergonomically correct."

But few of us really know what that phrase means. There is a knot of actual ergonomists out there who know, but their message is diluted by people passing themselves off as ergonomists. You can't really tell one from the other without an autopsy.

I had coffee with Phil Jacobs of St. Paul, current president of the local chapter of the national Human Factors & Ergonomics Society, and he brought me up-to-date with his whole misunderstood profession.

Ergonomics is a calling in the whirlwind. Well over half the things consultants are asked to be experts on didn't even exist ten years ago. In 1988, there were no VGA monitors, no laptops, no back-pocket PDAs; today everyone is up in arms over color screens, headaches, wooziness, aching kidneys, radiation output, etc. In such a fast-moving discipline, how much conclusive data can ergonomists have at their fingertips? And how long will even that small handful of data be relevant?

If you look in the Yellow Pages under Ergonomics, what you will see is mostly vendors for products that claim to have ergonomic benefits.

HOW TO LIFT YOUR COMPUTER

One of my first clients was a chiropractor of some renown, who told me that a chalky blur on my back X-rays was the result of drinking too much cream soda. But he also taught me how to lift things. Here is the gist of his advice, as applied to the problem of lifting a computer to take it to the repair shop.

Carry the computer in an embrace. That is to say, do not hold the computer out at arm's length. This puts tremendous strain on your sacroiliac. Nor should you bend over backward to accommodate its weight. This is impossible, and attempting it risks permanent musculoskeletal injury.

The correct way to lift a computer is to stoop down, bending at the knees—let those

(Continued on page 138)

legs do as much of the lifting work as possible—and hoisting the computer up to your chest. Pretend you love it—which may be difficult at this point. Hug it close to your chest, to optimize your center of gravity and to take the weight off your spine.

This embrace-lift is not easy, especially if you are angry at your computer for needing to be transported in the first place.

Other tips:

Unplug the computer manually. Trying to unplug it after you have lifted it is madness.

Plan ahead. Think about doors and what they might mean to your forward progress.

Get dressed first. Taking the computer out to your car naked risks social embarrassment, and the weight of a heavy CPU can leave a nasty and lasting impression on your skin.

The products may or may not be excellent; but if a company sells a certain product, chances are that's the product they will decide your company needs. And thus is born the fear of the $600 chair.

Some people passing themselves off as ergonomic consultants have no training at all in the field. What can a company do to assure that its ergonomist didn't work the previous week wrestling alligators?

First, steer clear of sales people masquerading as independent consultants. Second, look for credentials. A graduate degree in one of several areas is a must: industrial engineering, occupational medicine, safety, industrial psychology, occupational therapy, or physical therapy. Avoid degrees in mortuary science. Look for the credentialing initials after the consultant's name on his or her business card: CHPF for Certified Human Factors Professional, CPE for Certified Professional Ergonomist, or CSP for Certified Safety Professional.

WHAT YOU CAN DO

- **Read up.** Information on ergonomic health changes a lot from year to year. Court cases are setting and reversing precedents almost every month. Last year's great products don't always look so good a year later.
- **Take responsibility yourself.** Sad to say, you are the only person who really cares about your body. Companies still aren't awake to the possibility that their employees are going to sue them someday. Don't wait for them to look out for your well-being.

- **Know your type.** Different kinds of users suffer from different ailments, or the ailments result from different usage patterns. Technophiles suffer the most because they voluntarily put in more hours at the console. Technophobes get headaches out of sheer frustration. Worriers sometimes hold their mouse wrong, or their hands wrong—they need to remind themselves to relax this tension. (How about creating a Windows marquee saying "RELAX" or "COOL BREEZE"?) People persons get "phone receiver ear" from too much time on the phone. Whatever you are affects the way you use your machines.

- **Start with the right height chair.** Then adjust the rest of the office—keyboard, desk, monitor—to you. You should be able to put your feet on the floor, with your knees pointing slightly up. With chairs, big is not always best, and the chair needn't be adjustable. It should let you put your wrists at keyboard level, with your forearm at a right angle to your upper arm. The chair should support your lower back. Tip for shorter people: Raise the chair to put the wrists at keyboard level. Then use a foot rest to anchor your feet.

> "Quit worrying about your health. It'll go away."
>
> *Robert Orben*[6]

- **A clear, stable, readable image.** You need a good quality monitor. Ask for one with a low "dot pitch" of .26 or less. The lower the dot pitch, the tighter the image—the eye has to do less work imagining what the image is trying to be. Only you can decide what's best for your eyes—see the monitor in action before you buy. For better contrast and resolution, faster response, and smaller footprint, consider gray-scale over color VGA. Bright color is harder on the eyes than subdued color—make sure the monitor dials allow lots of adjustability.

- **Don't sit too close.** Sit as far from the monitor as you can and still work comfortably. Some businesses embed monitors in counters, so users must look down—this can be hard on many people's spines.

- **Take breaks.** Use your system clock alarm to signal 30-minute keyboard breaks. Get up, stretch out, walk around, blink. It doesn't seem productive, short term; long-term, it's a company-saver.

- **What a trip.** One of the biggest causes of on-the-job injury is people tripping on power cords. Get them out of the way.

- **What about radiation?** While users are concerned about screen emissions, the jury is still out on whether they do harm. If radiation concerns you, investigate TCO monitors like those from Nanao, costing $1,600–$2,000, or less costly radiation filters that can be fitted onto your current monitor.

- **Know where the radiation is coming from.** Most radiation exits from the back of your monitor. Back-to-back PCs increase radiation risk.
- **Keep a sponge handy.** Computer screens attract dust magnetically. Wipe your screen every few days, before the image starts to occlude.
- **A well-lit room.** Glare from room light and sunlight can be annoying and exhausting. Glare filters are available for $30 or less, but they can also cut image clarity. Lighting should come from the sides or above, not from in front or behind. Use window shades. Several soft light sources beat a single bright beam. If your light source is fixed in one place, move your desk and machine to get the best angle.

"It's a sure sign of summer if the chair gets up when you do."

Walter Winchell[7]

- **Use a computer desk.** The biggest mistake people make is putting a PC and keyboard atop a regular desk, forcing the user's hands and eyes higher than they should be. The goal is a desk that keeps your wrists low and your monitor at eye level. Those fiberboard desk kits for sale at office supply stores look gross and lack the drawer space of a good old-fashioned desk—but they are usually a bit lower and better suited to computer work.
- **Keep wrists relaxed and straight.** To prevent stress injury, keep your wrists straight. Check out the inexpensive ($10 and up) wrist rests and wrist supports. But don't press against them—pressing against a rest will exacerbate stress.
- **Keyboards should permit relaxed typing.** Piano teachers tell us how to hold our hands—but no one tells us how to type safely. Choose a keyboard that puts the hands in a natural position and does not require jabbing or squeezing.
- **Let the mouse roam free.** Mouse design is less important than room to roam. Give your mouse lots of rolling space, so you are not bumping up against things. Keep it beside the keyboard, not above it.
- **Use a good chair.** It doesn't have to be a $600 chair. You can fashion chairs, desks, typing stands, footrests, and tables out of materials salvaged from empty lots and dumpsters. It ain't pretty, but it won't

hurt you, either. A good chair should prevent pain, not cause it. It doesn't have to be adjustable, if its natural angle is right for you, and you are the only person who will sit in it.

- **Do other things.** I must exercise my hands, back, and eyes at least every half hour. Your hands especially love to work, provided the work is varied. Home computer users are at an advantage here. They can break to do some gardening, knead bread, whatever they enjoy. I have always wanted to try Hall of Fame pitcher Steve Carlton's Zen routine: plunging one's hands in tall buckets full of rice and flexing them with the rice pressing around them. There's even space for the buckets beside my desk.

- **Maintain good habits.** Remember the basic posture: feet flat on the floor, knees slightly up, back supported, elbows at right angles, and wrists straight. Give yourself frequent breaks to get up and walk around. Keep moving and stretching throughout the work day to alleviate tension and improve circulation. Exercise can help protect the most important apparatus equipment in your office—your body.

- **Get help.** As soon as you feel an ache, see your doctor. Ergonomic injuries are much easier to avoid or halt than they are to reverse.

CHAPTER ■ 8

Can the Earth Survive Computing?

Ecoschemes for Users Worried About the World

In which the rhetorical question is asked, What doth it profit a user of technology to gain access to the whole world, if that world is going to hell in a handbasket

One of the more comforting nostrums of the personal computer world is that they are, above all, clean. They use relatively little energy, they are not manufactured in smoke-belching factories, and people who use 'em, like telecommuters, often wind up conserving other resources—gasoline being the biggie.

Compared to cars—the only technology that can compare to PCs, in terms of influencing the way we live and think—computers seem almost spiritual. Life with computers has often implied a move away from the environmental shadows of the recent and current era. That has always been part of its allure—that the Age of Information, clean, pure, and unpolluted, would follow on the heels of and be the antidote to the Age of Soot. From the smokestack to the cleanroom.

It's easy to see why we feel that way. Computers just sit there and hum. They don't belch smoke or leak oil or emit odor. They don't drop their rusted parts along the shoulders of roads. But they still have significant negatives. On one obvious level there is the matter of paper. Computing was once thought to lead ineluctably to the paperless office—everything would be saved on disk, and accessed on monitors, with the rare printout for the feeble and old.

Even the newest, rawest computer recruit knows this hasn't come to pass. People who, Pre-Computer, got by on a half-ream of paper a year suddenly found themselves going through box after box of flat sheets or tractor-feed continuous forms. The solitary computer user may shrug and say that a big box of 3,500 sheets is no big deal. But multiply that box by the thirty million other home and small-business computerists, and then by the astronomical usage patterns of Fortune 500 companies and every other business, school,

> ## DESPOLIATION
> ### Paradox #8
> Systems designed to make the world a better place instead place the world in jeopardy.

and institution, and you see what sort of burden we are placing on our forests and landfills. Multiply that number, in turn, by the explosion in publishing and direct mail that computers have helped feed, and one understands why we are losing timberland at the rate of four square miles per day. Write a novel, kill an owl.

There are other problems as well. Inks, chemicals, and toners for printers are uniformly toxic. Chipmaking and floppy disk manufacture involve egregious amounts of etching acids, solvents, and other noxious petrochemicals. Monitors are an unsortable melange of plastic, glass, and steel. Computers use up valuable petrochemical feedstuffs, and when discarded, they sit around in closets and landfills, breathing trace amounts of toxic vapors, for virtually ever. The plastic film that floppies and their jackets are made from? There

> Thank God men cannot as yet fly and lay waste the sky as well as the earth.
>
> *Henry David Thoreau*[1]

are mountains of it out there in the world now, and the mountains keep growing.

Energy? True, small computers themselves do not use much more electricity than a hi-fi. The Apple II+ and IBM PCs came with modest little power supplies. But subsequent models came with bigger power units, fans, and storage drives. Their peripherals and support systems—printers, FAX machines, air-conditioning, lighting, and other add-ons—all cried out for more juice.

And anyway, the sheer number of machines plugged in around the globe is sufficient to exert a downward tug on our overall energy capacity, worsening air quality, straining landfills, and bleeding weird solvents into the water tables.

ATMOSPHERIC CHANGES

There is no environmental issue that raises as many hackles and politically polarizes people as much as the apparent destruction of our biosphere's outer ozone layer by chlorofluorocarbons (CFCs).

You may remember CFCs. They are the class of chemicals lumped together in headlines almost 20 years ago, when atmospheric chemists Sherwood Rowland and Mario Molina discovered that these chemicals, used as coolants in refrigeration and air conditioning units, as elements in foam products, and as propellants in spray cans, were somehow discombobulating stratospheric ozone 8 to 30 miles above our heads.

Until then hardly anyone knew or cared about what the ozone layer was. Now everyone knows that it is like a skin holding our atmosphere together, shielding us against harmful solar radiation. A protector of life, the ozone layer was itself the creation of life—formed billions of years ago by rotting oceanic life-forms. Without the ozone layer, the theory goes, we will be helpless against a wave of horrific plagues—skin cancer, crop failure, the extinction of thousands of species of plants and animals. CFCs also, it appears, speed up global warming and what comes with that—smog, flooded coastlines, and depleted timberlands.

> "I'll put a girdle round about the earth."
>
> *William Shakespeare*[2]

Unfortunately for environmentalists—and journalists—it is impossible to discuss such outcomes without sounding hysterical. Rush Limbaugh has a field day making scientists who fret about continued life on earth sound like white-coated Chicken Littles.

This despite a recent news report that an enormous iceberg, 30 miles by 50 miles across and 100 yards thick, has broken off from the James Ross Island ice shelf and is drifting northward as I type this. The news report said the floe may take 20 years to melt. I mention this not because I am afraid of icebergs but because it may illustrate the theory that the atmosphere is getting warmer. If that happens, lots of icebergs will be heading our way, even if we live in Kansas City.[3]

In the case of CFCs, the greatest damage is not being caused by nonsolvent (refrigerant) CFCs at all, but by solvent CFCs. Rowland did a map of the world and discovered that, while places like Alaska and Madagascar emitted zero CFCs, one place emitted them like nobody's business—Silicon Valley, California, home of Apple, Hewlett-Packard,

IBM, and a million other computer companies. High technology, wherever it exists around the world, is creating one huge spike in CFC activity after another. Single-handedly, the industry is pushing mammoth amounts of the stuff skyward.

Computer company CFCs more than erased any progress made by the abandonment of CFCs in hair sprays and refrigerators. In a controversial essay in *Mother Jones*,[4] environmental gadfly and Earth Day founder Dennis Hayes argued that the electronics industry not only knew all along about the damage it was causing but that it had viable CFC alternatives they could have used, but, like Bartleby the Scrivener, simply preferred not to. Dupont and Dow Chemical could do it, but Unisys, DEC, and Compaq could not.

There is no question that CFCs are wonderful solvents. Engineers love them because they pour out as a thick gas, penetrate through to the micropores of silicon chips, disk heads, and circuit boards—and then simply evaporate, leaving spanking clean hardware. Whereas refrigerant CFCs were designed to stay inside a tank for the life of the machine, solvent CFCs are supposed to escape—that is their purpose in life, to make cleanup a breeze. All through the boom years of the 1980s, computer companies poured on the CFCs like nobody's business, venting fumes into the open air. Only recently have the bigger companies installed emission traps.

WHO IS GENERAL FAILURE, AND WHY IS HE READING MY HARD DRIVE?

An error message is a short, cryptic statement your computer makes when it wants to shift blame from its programmers onto you. Here are some actual error messages:

Disk Error A)bort R)entry F)ail
Feb is not the name of a month.
General Protection Fault
Invalid Filename or File Not Found
File Allocation Table Error
Fatal Error—System Halted
Insufficient Resources
Insufficient memory—aborting . . .
System not responding . . .
Something bad happened and I
    don't know what it is. (Macintosh)
Drive C: No such drive.
Timed out while doing something
    indeterminable
Unable to Load Command Processor
What? (syntax error)
How? (operand error)
Sorry! (out of memory)
(WHAT, HOW, and SORRY were the
    only error messages on early
    TRS-80 systems)

(Continued on page 146)

ERROR MESSAGES YOU HOPE YOU NEVER SEE:

Access denied! Do something constructive for a change!

The nanobites are in full-scale rebellion.

SYSTEM ERROR 1303 : POWER NOT ON

There is NO way to do that!

HIT ANY KEY TO CONTINUE, when you've already hit EVERY key and things are locked up tighter than an old man after three pounds of cheese.

Deleting user. Computer needs no further input.

#6 ∧ (*&_) *) (bjklkuhkj76&∧* ( ) YG (%* ∧& (PG Not reading ready dr dr

dr dr dr ive C:

LPT1 on fire

You know, we all have our stereotypical images of what sort of people sit at the corporate boardrooms in Silicon Valley. Levi Dockers–types, with featherweight, wire-rimmed yuppie specs, interested in making a profit, sure, but every bit as interested in making the world a groovier place to raise kids and drive a Volvo station wagon. That's my stereotype—Apple Computer types.

These are the tuned-in dudes who, with all the evidence in the world amassed before their eyes that their solvents of choice were having a devastating effect on the planetary radiation shield, nevertheless pulled every trick in the book to avoid changing.

"The issue (of ozone depletion) was controversial among leading scientists and the data was inconclusive," says an internal IBM memo quoted in Hayes' book, *Behind the Silicon Curtain: The Seductions of Work in a Lonely Era.* This despite the fact that researchers Rowland and Molina had been profusely honored by the scientific community, including bestowal of the prestigious Japan Prize for Environmental Science and Technology. In 1979 the National Academy of Sciences announced findings showing that ozone loss was occurring even more rapidly than Rowland and Molina had projected. And it is said that today's measurable depletion represents effluents released 20 years ago—the recent junk hasn't even reached the big top yet.

The industry's mouthpiece group, the American Electronics Association, was handed even harder statements to deliver straight-faced. In 1989 testimony before a Senate environmental subcommittee, an AEA spokesperson said that CFCs were the unanimous choice of computer manufacturers because "they were believed to be environmentally benign, neither contributing to air pollution nor to any hazardous-waste problems."

The amount of CFCs dumped into our biosphere between 1979 and 1995 is estimated to surpass 15 billion pounds. The amount of ozone in the upper atmosphere, by contrast, is scant—its molecules scattered far apart in the low-gravity of near space. Passive, fragile, unfixable.

Today, the situation is somewhat under control. In 1987, 45 industrial and developing countries signed the Montreal Protocol on Substances that Deplete the Ozone Layer, an international pledge to phase out CFCs. Computer companies are in the uncomfortable position of publicly giving the Montreal Protocols lip service but working tirelessly behind the scenes to extend compliance deadlines and otherwise blunt the effort to eliminate the killer chemicals.

"We can't do it alone," appears to be the rallying cry. "Trying to reduce CFC emissions in the U.S. will have a negligible effect on ozone depletion," an AEA representative told Congress as it pondered regulations to implement the Montreal Protocol.

What makes this potentially tragic is that there was a perfectly satisfactory alternative solution to CFCs all along—essentially, water. Aqueous cleaning, using water and ultrasound, was the industry standard up until the late 1970s, when everyone switched to CFCs for their evaporation properties. And it's affordable. AT&T Bell Labs reported that switching to water-based cleaning systems would raise circuit-board manufacturing costs by all of 1 percent.

The other solution falls under the name of terpenes—organic cleaners that can be found in just about every living plant. Terpenes probably work even better than water and ultrasound and are noncorrosive and nontoxic. AT&T—one of the good guys in this grim little fable—uses a terpene product made from orange rinds and wood pulp. AT&T says it can switch immediately from CFCs to water and terpenes, while the rest of Silicon Valley begs for ten years' time to get its act together. After all, what's another billion pounds of CFC?

Eventually, the big manufacturers have come to see the light. In 1992 and 1993, Apple, Hewlett-Packard, and Compaq all announced that they would abide, finally, by the Montreal Protocols on abandoning CFCs. These announcements appeared as 100-word articles in *Infoworld*, *MacWeek*, and *PC Week*. You knew there were arguments at the boardroom level whether to boast of the achievement ("Buddies of the Earth") or let the matter sneak guiltily onto the record. Decency won out. Eventually, all the big companies here and abroad got behind the new move—IBM, Digital, Unisys, Sony, Matsushita, Mitsubishi. But good lord, this didn't happen until the 20 billion pounds of CFCs were already making their way to the polar ozone holes. And the low dollar shops in China, Korea, Mexico, and Singapore are still at it.

How does the world really work? It ain't your cards and letters and protests in the street. In the case of Hewlett-Packard, it was the fact that Chairman David Packard's daughter Julie ran the Monterey Bay Aquarium, and she was outspoken about it.

Way to go, Julie. Now if the rest of us can just exert the same powers of persuasion with our Silicon Valley billionaire dads. . . .

Solid Waste

My neighbor had just gotten back from a trip out East and was eager to tell me about it.

"I was walking down some street on the Lower East Side, and there it was, just sitting out with the trash—the CPU and keyboard for an XT clone. So I toted it back to the van and brought it home. Some find, huh?"

It sure was, I told him. What was he going to do with it? It couldn't run today's software, and my neighbor wouldn't be content running 10-year-old programs.

He looked at me impatiently, as if I were focusing on negatives. The important thing was that he had saved a perfectly good machine from an ignominious fate in some landfill in New Jersey, perhaps within arm's reach of Jimmy Hoffa.

And there the matter stands. There are 75 million PCs out there, all aging rapidly. Every year, 10 million are put out to pasture. Put them all in a pile, where they will all be in ten years, and we will have a mountain of about 6 million tons—an acre in breadth, three and a half miles deep, room to stack 15 Empire State Buildings end to end. That's more than your average Adirondack.

Prices on PCs keep tumbling as new PCs become even more powerful, robbing older PCs of value. Yet, like my neighbor's foundling, these old boxes still seem too "valuable" to throw away. Is there anything you can do with them?

The ideal answer is not to recycle the computer but to reuse it somehow. There are a couple of obvious ways to do this—hand the computer down to a younger family member, or donate it to a school. But are you really doing anyone a favor, giving them a free XT? Kids need what new computers offer—good graphic interfaces—more than adults do. And the software those old computers run is awfully musty.

In a school setting, it's hard to claim you're preparing a child for the future by sitting them down at a relic of the past. The bottom line is the same as it was for the XT on the Manhattan curbside: the space it takes up is more valuable than the work it can do.

So what are your options? You can sell it to a college student. A low-end XT system can still bring $250 on the open market.

There are also used computer brokers that will take it off your hands, and pay you perhaps $100 for it. Then they will package it with a lot of similar systems and sell it to a school system, or even better, on the global secondary market, where a boring old (to us) PC represents a quantum leap forward in technology.

A nonprofit agency that delivers last year's technology to this year's developing nations is the East West Development Foundation in Boston (617-542-1234), which distributes computers to over 130 nations. So your old PC may wind up crunching numbers in Quito or Monrovia.

You may also be able to use your computer as a bargaining chip when you upgrade. If you buy from a consultant or repair group, chances are good that they will take the computer off your hands, subtract a few hundred dollars from the purchase price of your new system, and then use their own contacts to find a place for your old system—with a school or charity, or lumping it in with a bundle of machines headed for Pakistan.

A better idea may be to find a secondary use for the machine. Old PCs can't run the latest Windows or CD-ROM programs, but they are

> **1972.** Hewlett Packard creates the HP-35 Electronic Slide Rule. The first pocket calculator. It could solve, in one minute, what it took a regular slide rule five minutes to do.
>
> **1972.** Nolan Bushnell introduces Pong, the first electronic arcade game, for Atari machines. It is a smash hit.
>
> **1972.** The dedicated word processor, the invention of Wang Laboratories, is unveiled to large corporations, revolutionizing secretarial pools. The earliest models had no monitor—they were just typewriters with cassette drives for storage. Expensive and clunky, the Wang Word Processing System was how many people first encountered computing.

perfectly adequate for certain dedicated tasks in the home or office—turning lights on and off, adjusting the thermostat, keeping an eye on your home security system or garage door opener, monitoring incoming calls, serving as a hub for your answering machine, voicemail, or fax machine. I, for example, use a separate, slower machine for my Internet calls.

Sure, your newer computer can do these things, too. But as we all know, as wonderful as multitasking is, these tasks still have a way of tripping over one another and crashing. A dedicated system to handle the most volatile chores is a good way to sidestep these conflicts.

Perhaps the commonest use old PCs are put to is running a computer bulletin board system (BBS). There are thousands of homegrown BBSes out there today, and nearly all of them run on secondhand systems. The reason is that processing time—the downfall of the old 8086 and 80286 chips—is practically irrelevant in telecommunications, which are already limited by (usually) much slower modem transmission times.

Why would you want to start a BBS? For one thing, because it's fun. I know a dozen people who, with no special technical backgrounds, have added a gratifying dimension to their otherwise gray and meaningless lives by starting up chat boards. The BBS is simply a way for like-minded individuals to get together, read one another's thoughts, and respond.

BBSing is seductive. When you start, you see it as a cold, faceless medium. But with the passage of time you come to number these faceless people among your closest friends.

You can also use your BBS as a kind of network for a home business or hobby. Your colleagues, clients, dealers, and customers can communicate with you through your own private e-mail system, leaving short notes or uploading huge files. And all you need is an old computer and a phone line.

You can also use your PC as the front end for a ham radio set-up. Most amateur radio involves voice transmission, like a phone, but a great deal of it is digital—coded messages that sound like blips and squeaks to the ear but can easily be decoded and responded to using a PC with a shortwave converter. Once you get your amateur's license, you can convert all sorts of interesting data—messages from other operators, weather stations, and news organizations around the world.

If that's not esoteric enough, how about using the computer as a robotic brain? Robotics are ultra-sophisticated kinetic task repeaters—but they aren't especially smart or fast. You can buy robotics kits from the back pages of electronics magazines, and there are several fun books on the market that can help you get started making robots either for some practical use or as toys.

If efforts to reuse the computer come to naught, true recycling—dismantling the machine and redirecting its components for reuse or scrap—is possible, but not easy.

A New Jersey company called Advanced Recovery has led the way in computer recycling. The small firm handles about 20 tons of computer gear every month. But it's not as simple as crushing a car into a 3-foot cube. Computer components range widely in value and utility. Recyclers must take each box apart, first setting aside any items that can be resold as is—modems, expansion cards, mice, keyboards, monitors, etc. The chips are extracted and sold to parts wholesalers and repair shops.

Those items that cannot be reused must then be broken down. First the computer is mined for metals, which include aluminum, copper, and gold. The steel cabinets are removed and sold as scrap. Even some plastic resins can be stripped for recycling. Whatever is left is then carted off to the landfill.

The problem with all this commodity harvesting is that it is slow, painstaking work that no one is making much money doing. Recycled plastic is cheaper than virgin resin by the ounce, but not if it takes you all day to pick it out of your computer innards. The older the machine you own, the more difficulty you will have separating out the savables.

The good news is that, in years to come, computers will be designed with recycling in mind. If companies don't make it easy through modular design, snap-apart connections, and—as much as possible—single-material construction, they will have to assume the cost for landfilling themselves, in the form of some kind of environmental levy.

Under the strict "take-back" regulations in effect in Germany, computer companies are compelled by law to take back computers that users no longer want. With such a law on the books, a dozen recycling companies have sprung up to seek profits in amongst the red tape. It's doubtful that the U.S. will go to such a mandatory system, but computer companies know that the federal government will not tolerate a new generation of PC junkyards on the outskirts of every town.

Though every computer maker from Apple to Zeos has voiced support for a greener PC, IBM has taken the lead in actual recycling. The company has already opened recycling centers in New Haven, CT, and Raleigh, NC, and has announced intentions to establish more across the country for users to bring their unwanted machines to.

It's Not Easy Being Green

How hard is it to "be good" environmentally? To glance at the book covers (*101 Ways to Save the Earth*), it's easy—you just do the 101 things.

In reality it's very hard. You aren't screwing up the planet much; we as a civilization, all together, are. The things you can do as an individual don't stack up to much. And some of them are nearly impossible. Like recycling vinyl just can't be done in my home town of St. Paul, for instance. I'd have to mail my vinyl to Chicago. And I'm sorry, Mother Earth, but I refuse to do that.

> "We can lick gravity, but the paperwork will be overwhelming."
>
> *Werner von Braun*[5]

Consider a seemingly simple task—getting the postman to deliver less junk mail to your office or home every day. It's a worthy ambition: every year you get a tree's worth of junk mail. Get that tree down from a mighty oak to a slender sapling, and you'll be doing the earth a favor. Not to mention your postal person.

But it is a daunting task, involving hours at your word processor and sending lots of (you got it) unwanted letters. There is no central clearinghouse for mail lists that you can write to. The company that sent you junk isn't the problem so much as the company that sold that company your name. Companies that mail to you buy their lists from outside, often on a one-time use basis. So they have no way to clean the lists beforehand, even though they should want to keep your catalog out of the recycling bin. If you want to stop getting the mail, you have find out who they buy names from and get those people to stop selling your name.

One thing you can easily do is write the Direct Marketing Association (11 West 42nd Street, New York, NY 10163-3861), the direct mailer trade organization. They have a kit you can use to notify the industry of your feelings. This doesn't work as well as it should though—you might want to re-notify them every six months.

The problem is, there are dozens of ways list-sellers can get your name and address. When you do business with them, you have no idea that their hidden agenda is in adding you to the lists they sell. The primary culprits include:

Mail order companies. When you buy an item by mail, the vendor resells your name to businesses selling complementary products. Thus, if you bought luggage, you may end up on a travel list. A good practice is to use a variant of your name, title, or street address—Michael A. Finley. Michael B. Finley, Michael C. Finley, etc.—with each vendor. That way, when you start getting offers, you know who's been selling your name, and ask them to stop it. Most companies will add your name to a special "suppression" list.

Credit cards. These folks know more about your spending habits than you do. Use a special name for each card. If a company refuses to suppress your name, send back their plastic.

Groups you thought were your friend. Churches, professional associations, etc. Selling names is a quick way to raise extra money. It may seem strange giving them all different names, but it's the best way to find out who's selling you out.

The phone book. With the advent of CD-ROM phone directories, any business can merge and purge its own mail list. Sometimes just the exchange, or the block you live on, or your name, will tell them what they need to know. Again, you could pick a fake name for the directory—but you have to tell everyone your fake name. The other possibility is getting an unlisted number.

Product registration cards. Yup, companies have an ulterior motive in collecting these. Usually they are sent to the National Demographics and Lifestyles Company (attn: List Order Department, 1621 18th St., Suite 300, Denver, CO 80202), which culls information you entered yourself and sells lists based on what you said. Write them and ask them not to include you on their lists.

"Occupant" mail. You get all those circulars, oil change coupons, missing children ads from local merchants. The national ADVO ("Mailbox Values") and Harte Hanks ("Potpourri"). Keeping this sort of mail at bay is tough. You have to call their local sales office, tell them to stop printing your card, then hassle your post office to stop delivering it even without the card, which is illegal. Once they know you're a nut about this, they'll stop.

By now you've got the idea. To cut down on computerized mail overload you have to generate a lot of computer mail of your own. It would be nice if simpler measures worked, but they don't:

Complaining via the business's own Business Reply Envelopes (BREs). This mail goes to a different planet (order redemption) than you want (customer service). They'll just circular file it.

Attaching a brick to a BRE. The post office is on the lookout for this sort of thing. There's a stack of undelivered bricks out in Wyoming somewhere that's so big that air traffic must be routed around.

If you're really serious about undertaking this effort and want the complete lowdown, dial on to the Internet, go to the Usenet **alt.answers** newsgroup, and download a file called Junk Mail FAQ (Frequently Asked Questions) by Chris Hibbert. I got most of my ideas from that document, and it includes a ton of addresses and other ideas. It's free.

If all this fails, you have the option of pulling up stakes and moving, and leaving no forwarding address. But you can't tell anyone (including creditors, employer, insurers, old friends, and most especially the Post Office).

> **processor**—This is the part of the computer that does what computers do. Just as a food processor mills vegetables, a data processor mills information. A microprocessor is a very little one.
>
> **real estate**—The amount of desktop space available to the user's elbows.
>
> **snailmail**—The United States Postal Service.

RECYCLE YOUR FLOPPIES?

When you got your first hard disk, you were suddenly the owner of those dozens of 5¼-inch floppies that you had been using for data backup. Then, when you switched to 3½-inch floppies, you came into an even larger hoard of old floppies. You saw this at the time as a windfall. Now, years later, you realize you are stuck with a hundred or so floppies that you will never be able to use.

Help may be on the way. GreenDisk Co. of Redmond, WA, has announced plans to take old floppies, demagnetize and reformat them, and then resell the freshly cleaned media at a fraction of the cost of new floppies. GreenDisk has even found a way to recycle Tyvek envelopes—previously considered unrecyclable.

For the moment, GreenDisk is concentrating on refurbishing disks used by large software companies who go through millions of disks every year. But the effort will keep hundreds of tons of plastic out of landfills—and, if successful, we can expect to see small regional operators jumping to cash in on the opportunities. That's when you can finally unload that big box of diskettes.

The next logical step, CD-ROM and circuit board recycling is also in the works, but the average user won't benefit from them for a while. Best advice: take all your junk to your repair partner. They go through a lot of computer junk. If there is money to be made trading these old materials, or saved by keeping them out of the local landfill, they will know.

WHAT INDUSTRY MUST DO

Complete the switch from CFCs to terpenes or aqueous-based solvents. Don't just do it yourself; require your suppliers to do it, too. Even your suppliers in countries with negligible environmental regulations.

Emphasize environmental aspects in advertising. Sure, price is important to us, but saving a buck doesn't do us much good if we live in a toxic waste dump.

When crises occur, meet them head-on. One more 20 megaton denial circus like we saw with CFCs, and the industry's credibility on environmental matters is toast.

WHAT YOU SHOULD DO IN THE MEANTIME

Do three things. Forget the *101 Things You Can Do to Save the Earth*. Find three valid activities that you know you can do, and do those. Here are a few that seem worthwhile to me:

- **Look for the Energy Star.** These EPA-sanctioned components use a "sleep mode" to automatically power down when not in use. To qualify as Energy Star–compliant, monitors must be able to power down to 30 watts or less when not in use. You can install Energy Star components to old machines so that they can save, too. Note: powering up and down takes time. You may want to set your parameters for powering down broadly so it isn't going up and down every five minutes.

- **Use fluorescent lights.** They glare less, use less heat, cause fewer fires, and almost never burn out. Less time standing on rickety chairs screwing in light bulbs means increased productivity.

- **Work from the screen.** Many of us print out a dozen or a score of drafts to peruse before printing the "final" version. Learn to edit from the screen. Forget blue-penciling and Post-It Notes and change text directly on-screen. With today's WYSIWYG word processors and spreadsheets there is no need for all those paper drafts.

- **Use the power switch.** It used to be popular, especially among home office types, who may feel the urge to compute at any hour of the day, to leave PCs on 24 hours a day; it minimized the shock of booting up, and in a small office the cost was not much. But with today's larger systems, and bigger networks, cost is a huge factor: if your company has 150 PCs, just turning off the color monitors at night can save you $17,000 a year in electricity costs.[70] Personally, I compromise—I turn the monitors and printers off at night, and leave the CPU on.

- **Repair.** Too often we upgrade to another machine or tool because our current one is on the fritz. Why spend $100 on repairs on our old whatsit when, for $175, you can get a brand-new whatsit that is faster and has blinking lights? That is often compelling logic, but every now and then it pays to fix the old one and keep it out of the waste stream.

- **Rent.** You probably don't need a full-page color scanner more than a few times a year. Instead of buying one and taking up the resale, disposal, storage, and repair headaches that go with ownership, why not rent or lease one?

- **Reuse.** Use it for tasks that are less mission-critical—kids' homework or home security. Or set it out on your curb and see what enterprising soul sees the value and makes off with it. If you're done with a PC, and it is usable, donate it to a church, school, or thrift shop. For help placing your unwanted PCs, contact the Computer Recycling Center in Mountain View, CA (415-428-3700), or the National Cristina Foundation in Greenwich, CT (203-622-6000), or the East West Foundation in Boston (617-542-1234).

■ **Recycle.** These days an awful lot can be recycled. Rechargeable batteries, floppy disks, toner cartridges, and certainly the mountains of waste paper you create. Call your local recycling authority and find out what they'll pick up and what you can bring in yourself. On your product registration cards, there's usually a comment line. Take advantage of the honeymoon that exists between you and the manufacturer. Ask them, "When I'm done with this thing, how do I get rid of it?" If they really value you, they'll think of something.

CHAPTER ■ 9

How Technology Makes Liars of Us All

The Effect of Computers on Character

Confronting the theory that computers cheapen our characters, plus thoughts on plagiarism, pathological liars, piracy, and feeble efforts at humor; concluding with a moral fable about self-delusion

I t is a cliché of the digital life, one especially favored by professors in the humanities, that technology exerts an inexorably dehumanizing effect on people. It cuts us off from one another, separates us into little computing islands, makes us forgetful, narcissistic, self-involved, and our social skills atrophy until no one wants to be our friend.

What gets me about these antitechnology screeds is that the authors seem to think that just because they are steeped in the wisdom of what it means to be human, the world will screech its brakes and rethink its course. Like philosophers influence buying decisions. "I know, I'll write a passionate essay that is pro-humanity and anti-computer, and people will pay attention."

The arguments made against the machine age are often elegant and ingenious. Basically, they boil down to something like *Computer technology dazzles us with speed and fireworks while it ineluctably cheapens the human spirit.* They dilute the humanness of our work, our relationships, and our very being. Before we are "computed," we are people. Once we are computed we are numbers and never quite as human again. At least, that's the theory.

Computers impede our growth as human beings, they say.[1] Here's the argument: People already are the slowest maturing creature in all nature. While we grow, we learn, but only when immersed in the correcting atmosphere of the real world. Computers suck children into a virtual world that does not correct them; thus they don't learn needed life skills and thus they stay children longer. One thinks of grown adults who order their entire lives around their PC—its games, networks, hacking possibilities, etc.—to confirm this theory of stunted development. Can you think of anyone you know who really likes computers and seems stunted?

> ## DECEPTION
> Paradox #9
>
> Technology cannot lie, but it can easily make a liar out of you.

Not having fingers, computers are not even human enough to count the human way, in 10s, the humanists complain. Instead they created their own weird binary math, in which everything in the cosmos is reduced to some indecipherable permutation of 1s and 0s. You can write a poem on a Pentium, play Scriabin on a digital compact disc, or bit-map Van Gogh's "Sunflowers." But the masters are not mocked. The art is clever and remarkable but it is wrong. It is still just 1s and 0s a computer fashioned into a facsimile of the real thing. Computers cheapen everything. Dialog becomes dialog boxes. Icons—images of the unutterably beautiful—become little pictures you bop with a mouse. Human beings become numbers, files, codes.

> "Technological society has succeeded in multiplying the opportunities for pleasure, but it has great difficulty in generating joy."
>
> *Pope Paul VI*[2]

One observation academic technophobes make is that technology inevitably brings out the seamier side of human nature. Big technology—radio, TV, database networks, direct mail—enables the powerful to monitor and manipulate the less powerful. Local technology—your desktop PC, printer, phone, and fax modem— enables the less powerful to masquerade as the more powerful.

The technophobe sees technological progress as human devolution. George Orwell's *1984*, with its telescreens mounted in every room, was predicated upon the tyranny of machines. The shrinking attention span and declining test scores of young people today is seen as the consequence of a lifetime of noisy, disrespectful indoctrination—bad TV, bad music, the use of technology as a baby-sitter.

This devolution is echoed in the devolution of language. Things that had rich, deep meanings in regular English become tinpot analogs in Computer English. Logic in English is an elegant methodology for evaluating the truth and validity of human discourse; logic to a computer is merely an extension of algebra. A string search was a way to while away a rainy evening at home with the children; now it is a Boolean command statement. A monitor was something very still that watched you; now it is something very still that you watch.

I was at a business conference in Minneapolis recently where Tony Athos, co-author of *The Art of Japanese Management* and a classic curmudgeon, laid it on the line: "Computers degrade everything. We talk of cyberspace as if it were real space, and it isn't." Things that are called virtual generally are not—not really. A virtual community is light years from being a true community. No one would want a virtual dog. The things that we prize in life are the intangibles that resist digitization—and that cumulatively comprise a soul.

> "At the source of every error which is blamed on the computer you will find at least two human errors, including the error of blaming it on the computer."
>
> *Anonymous*[3]

So what does that make those of us who use and even like using technology? Two-dimensional, second-rate batch-run liars? Does our character corrode during our time at the console? It's a blunt accusation, but it doesn't come out of left field. The great delight of office technology is that it allows humble entities like ourselves to masquerade as something bigger, grander, richer. The PC is, in a very real sense, a fantasy machine, a fashioner of another reality, in which we can do or say things we otherwise would never do or say.

Using word processing, a desktop publishing system, and a purchased mailing list, it's a cinch to send out letters, brochures, catalogs, or even mount a World Wide Web home page that not only presents our one-person, down-on-its-luck organization as occupying the top half of an 80-story building and employing 900 people but allows us to address individual customers as if each one were our personal best friend.

But the fantasy is a lie. The "bigger, grander, richer" is all illusion. It's bad enough that we fool our customers, but we seem to be fooling ourselves as well. Technology augments not only our throughput but our hubris as well. It creates distance, encourages a kind of solitary narcissistic splendor, and lulls us into forgetting that our tasks had human goals.

Have you noticed you are getting more wrong numbers in the past few years than you did 20 years ago? The reason is technological: Touch-tone phones allow more rapid dialing than the old rotary dials. Our fingers move too quickly because the machine allows them to. Result: wrong connections, and rude, hasty hang-ups.

Another telephonic example is dialers. Many people now carry personal phone lists of 200 or more names and numbers with them, or they have them ready on-line for quick use. The result is that we have stopped memorizing phone numbers, even of our friends and families. It's so easy to have that list handy that we have abdicated from the business of remembering. Quick—what was the phone number of the last place you lived?

1975. The Altair 8800 Microcomputer is the first "personal computer," offered in kit form by a company in New Mexico called MITS. It was just a CPU with switches—no keyboard, no storage, no programs, and only enough memory to contain a couple dozen lines of code. But hobbyists went nuts for it, and it set the stage for the Apple II.

1975. Two guys in Seattle buy a tiny little operating system, buff it up a little, and sell it to Altair. Their names are Bill Gates and Paul Allen.

1976. Gary Kildall develops CP/M, the operating system that ruled the world until IBM tapped Gates' MS-DOS for its new personal computer. The choice of Microsoft over Kildall's Digital Research was one of the epochal moments in PC history. Legend has it that when IBM came calling, Kildall was out flying his airplane. Digital Research, acquired later by Novell, would seek some measure of revenge with its clone operating system DR-DOS.

Have you noticed you are getting more word-processed "family letters" during the holidays, and fewer handwritten letters? My family creates this kind of family letter, and we make no pretense that it is a handwritten 19th century epistle. It's basically a form letter to people we like, containing six paragraphs about the triumphs and trials of our family and its individual members, plus a single, solitary mail-merged sentence unique to the recipient ("We often think of you and Dell and that crazy escapade in the air shaft").

Most people enjoy it. But a few let us know in subtle ways that they feel "thinged" by the technology, that getting this kind of mail confuses them emotionally: they appreciate the thought but wish it were a real thought. One exasperated artist friend told me if he ever got another "machine letter" from me, our friendship was over.

What can I say? Holiday times are busy. We have two young children, as greedy as all get out, and lights to hang, and cookies to bake. We celebrate both Hannukah and Christmas and it's one big mess. Think of the family letter as automated goodwill. But by such fine shadings does the pearl lose its luster.

The ethical degradation is everywhere you look. It is in the decreased quality of products and services. It is in the falsely personal tone of marketing materials. It is in the false exclusivity of communications ("*Mr. Fred Flam of Canoga Park, you are in our final circle of $10,000,000 winners!*"). It is in the deteriorating condition of intellectual property laws—copyrights, patents, antiplagiarism, antipiracy, etc. It has forced us to create monstrous truth-detecting security systems that are straight out of *1984*. It so confuses us that we don't even know anymore when we are telling the truth.

Once again we see a techno myth following the one-size-fits-all pattern. Technology isn't out to deliberately degrade us. It has no satanic desires to corrupt humanity. I don't think.

And it obviously doesn't turn us all into the same degraded thing, or we would all be the same degraded thing. It does alter us; or to put blame where it belongs, it invites us to alter ourselves, according to what we already are.

The power user gradually stops trying to impress other people and burrows into his own nerdy infatuation with the machine. A few techno naturals become cruel and remote ("Puny earthlings!"). The earnest learner eventually masters what she sets out to learn, and her newfound sense of accomplishment and comfort with technology may make her a little smug. The dreamer who attains technological felicity makes it part of his private obsession, disappearing for long hours behind the screen. Even the plugger is changed, from being driven by necessity to the turf attitude that "I work hard at this, and I'm not about to let you make it any harder."

Technology picks us up, flips a few dipswitches on us, and sets us down again as slightly different people, in a slightly different world. Before technology our world was like a barnyard, with all the farm creatures wandering around primitively, interacting face to face. It was funkily charming. Post-technology, the world is more like a confinement facility on a modern egg farm. Each of us is in a separate box. We can cluck to our heart's content, and the other chickens can hear us and cluck back. But we never see one another, we are artificially inseminated, our food is chemically treated, and it's been ages since any of our eggs were allowed to hatch the way nature planned. We tell one another it's great to live in the modern age, but we privately pine for the days of fresh-air scratch and grunt.

Plagiarism Is Not a Beach

I was having lunch with an editor of a major national magazine a while ago, and we were rhapsodizing about the Internet. The only downside I saw to it, as a writer, was that it was bound to disintegrate existing copyright and other intellectual property laws.

If I decide to put a chapter of a book up, for feedback or just to show off, what's to stop some fellow from downloading it, nicking the © symbol off, and passing it off as his own?

The editor disagreed. He knew his employer had an army of lawyers ready to sic on any net-surfer who so much as looked at their data the wrong way. I lifted my coffee cup to him and hoped it would never be an issue for either of us.

But it's already too late. People are stealing so much so often and so heedlessly that half of them aren't even aware that it is theft. A respected *Chicago Sun-Times* editorial writer, Mark Hornung, resigned when it was revealed that an editorial of his about the balanced budget amendment contained five sentences more or less verbatim from a *Washington Post* editorial.

It was a painful disgrace for him, but I can imagine exactly how it happened. He started to write his own editorial, got stuck, downloaded a half dozen editorials from other papers to see what other people were saying, saw one he liked, block-moved it to his own on-screen document, and told himself that he would play with the text the next day and paraphrase it until it was "his own." But he got busy, or struck his head, and never made the appropriate changes to the borrowed text.

I am doing the exact same thing right now, looking at an Associated Press newsclip on the Hornung affair that I plucked from the net so I could get my facts right here. Unless I give the AP credit (which I hereby do), I'm swimming in the same broth as Mr. Hornung.

I guess I have always been pretty relaxed about plagiarism. For years I thought the word came from the French *plage*, for beach. I thought if you picked up a seashell and took it home, that was plagiarism. It turns out the correct root is the Latin *plagium*, for kidnapping. That's—very different.

Anyway, textfile importation is not the way we like to think journalism is committed, but it's not that far from standard operating procedure. Editorialists aren't gods. They're not burning with pre-set opinions, just waiting for an issue to walk by so they can stomp it to death. At least, I hope not. It is more likely that they are people who have to study up a lot to sound competent on a formidably wide spectrum of issues. It's their job to know what the *Post, Times,* and *Carbuncle-Procurer* are saying.

> "The search for technological progress is no longer a means, but has become an end in itself, escaping from human control and dominating man, alienating us from ourselves, our society, and our environment."
>
> *Vartan Gregorian, President of Brown University*[4]

It's pleasant to affect the air of being omniscient, but in fact everyone is working hard and running scared. To wake up one morning and find yourself in your own paper's headlines is every journalist's worst nightmare.

It is not the technology's fault, exactly. What Hornung did was lazy and stupid and, by definition, unoriginal. His fault all the way. But computer technology encourages us to make liars of ourselves. Think of it as entrapment. By being so fast and so powerful and so impressive, computers allow us to sound like much more than we are.

So a one-person company can put out documents as high-quality as Exxon. Some fly-by-night law firm can antagonize 70 million Internet users instantaneously with the touch of a key. Or an editorialist can inhale a statement by another paper and exhale one of his or her own that is only a little different. It is shabby, and we are all doing it to some degree.

You know what is the worst part, though? It's that technology drives up the expectations employers and customers have of us. With that PC, fax modem, laser printer, and scanner in front of you, sure, you can do the work six people did a decade ago. Your employer then uses that productivity gain to trim the workforce, maybe including people that used to check on you to make sure you didn't "exceed parameters" on ethics or quality.

So there you are, working yourself till you are blithering, without supervision or collaboration, and sooner or later your judgment falters, or you take an ugly shortcut, and your career takes a sharp turn to the southwest.

But all that time you were spinning like a dervish, delivering the value of six employees, you were never paid like six employees. You were paid like one well-paid employee. Period.

OK, maybe it's not Oliver Twist, but it's still a little poignant, isn't it? I'm not blaming employers, either. Everyone's trying their best to compete. In a global economy there's no place to hide, thanks to you-know-whats.

THE AGE OF EXCUSES

There is nothing as precious as a good excuse, and technology gives us a million of them.

Kids are the best excuse-makers, because kids need excuses more than anyone. Not only do you mess up a lot, but so many conditions of your existence truly are outside your control. If your pet pit bull decides to maul your book report with his rear cuspids, there's not much you can do about it.

Already, kids in the information age are making the necessary adjustments.

> Lightning hit our house and our surge suppresser failed to suppress the surge. Boy, is Dad disappointed.
>
> My sister tipped my Big Gulp onto the keyboard.
>
> I hit the wrong button when I saved it. I hope hexadecimal is OK.
>
> The only font that was working in Windows was Cyrillic.
>
> I did the assignment but we ran out of continuous feed paper, so I wasn't able to print it.
>
> Squirrels nibbled through our trunk lines.

Dad installed a compression utility last week and Mom says we won't be using the computer for a long time now.

I accidentally copied the first draft, which was 1000 words long, over the final draft. So now I'm short about 980 words. My mom said it was real good, though. You could call her. But she's in Japan.

The Mailer-Daemon returned my e-mail. Here's sixty lines of headers showing how my homework got stacked up over The Seychelles by a rogue asynchronous network router.

Your fax machine wouldn't shake hands with my fax machine. (See, it's almost your fault.)

> "Ther n' is no werkman whatever he be, That may both werken wel and hastily. This wol be done at leisure parfitly."
>
> *Chaucer*[5]

I count five separate sets of excuses. The first, and most reliable, is acts of God—the dog ate it, lightning knocked out a substation near my home, I booted up and my entire hard disk was mysteriously erased. There's not much people can say to this sort of excuse, so long as they aren't everyday occurrences, in which case you may need a note from your parents.

The second type is system failure: something that was supposed to work didn't. The .INI file was corrupt, the battery died, the electrons were stale, etc. This type of excuse works well—everyone appreciates this kind of frustration.

The third is design failure: something that was supposed to allow you to do work instead destroyed it: a faulty File Manager feature, bad docs, a print function that mysteriously erases files instead. It wasn't your fault, it was some nerd committee in Cupertino's.

A fourth wrinkle is the brand name excuse. I bought a clone instead of an IBM. My Pentium was a fake. God help me, I didn't choose AT&T (or FedEx, or The Club). Thinking people will not accept this excuse, but you may be able to coax the corporation into paying you for the testimonial.

Finally—and this is a cutting-edge excuse, not universally accepted as yet—there is the excuse by dismissal. My computer was down—you didn't expect me to do this assignment by hand, did you? I left my calculator in my other shirt pocket. The only word processor available to me was DOS-based. These excuses carry considerable weight with those who share your computing values—but may fall flat with the when-I-was-your-age set.

And they are the problem. Clearly, the proposition that nothing is ever your fault will raise the hackles of personal responsibility mavens. There will be editorials, there will be call-in programs, there will probably be multimedia CD-ROM workshops, all addressing the issue of our age: What can be done about creeping excusism?

To them we proffer the best excuse of all:

Hey, we didn't ask to be born.

Stolen Wares

Thanks to Michael Fay, we have come to think of Singapore as a no-nonsense place where malefactors are quickly impressed with the rule of law. Or is it the yardstick of law.

But there's more. Singapore, Malaysia, China, and even Vietnam are hives of software piracy. You can go into any software store in Singapore and a clerk will direct you to pirated copies of Lotus 1-2-3, (which retails here for $225), priced at about a dollar a disk.

Not a lot of end users are exercised about software piracy. There is a sense among many people that the software industry has helped cause the erosion of its own intellectual property efforts. Disks are easy to copy, data to download, scan. Protection schemes have long since been abandoned. How can low-tech police efforts quell all the high-tech swapping on?

Part of the vitality of our age is an outlaw attitude toward the old rules. If you think about it, technology is all about defying rules and the primacy of the individual. Rock and roll attitude, rock and roll technology.

The shareware phenomenon—legally downloading software programs for evaluation purposes—adds to the somewhat childish insistence that tools should be free. The fast lane of swapping and copying is the technological equivalent of rock and roll.

I have in my hands—no, now I'm putting it down—a weighty press kit from the Software Publishers Association. The SPA is the software industry's main trade association and also the entity entrusted with the task of nabbing pirates worldwide. The SPA describes four classes of piracy:

1. **Counterfeiting, Singapore-style**—duplicating the programs and packaging of a product.

2. **Hard disk loading**—where your computer dealer fills your disk with goodies, to seal the sale.

3. **Modem piracy**—where you download a copy of Microsoft Word from your local bulletin board.

4. **Less piratical license infractions**—but still painful to the industry—include businesses buying one copy of WordPerfect and installing it on 100 machines, and the common practice of friends sharing software.

Now, I know a lot of people who are not brought to tears at the thought of Bill Gates beset, Gulliverlike, by a swarm of Singaporean pirates and American teenagers. In fact, they downright cotton to the idea.

Gates and the software industry have been selling packages of paper and plastic for about $150 a pound now for 15 years. Software is a $60 billion industry worldwide. Gates pays an entire division just to peel his grapes. Who's ripping off whom? Where are the victims of software piracy?

Well, the software industry hires a lot of people, and they are not burger flippers. By any measure, it is one of the few industries in which the U.S. has a secure foothold and that provides lots of high-paying jobs. European software is a topic for polite tittering, and Japan is still playing catch up with us.

Piracy is especially invidious to smaller software companies that have sunk everything into a single product. That product may have the potential to succeed in a free market and even take on the big companies and their code-heavy standards. But not if its revenue stream is choked off at birth in a market of thieves.

Second, for every copy of a program that is stolen, the price of the regular version must inch upward a tiny bit. Development costs are inescapably high and must be paid by the only party that can pay for such things—us. Development costs are why the paper and plastic costs so much. Piracy only adds to the per-unit cost.

Now, it could be argued that business software in the last three years has been driving the greatest productivity increase in U.S.

business since the cotton gin—gains achieved, in part, thanks to "free" software. Few managers are fired for seeking out corner-cutting economies. So pirated programs are good for the economy as a whole, right?

But that's rationalization. I confess, I have swapped programs with friends in the past. Then I used those programs to make money. In my mind, I couldn't afford to buy a new copy of Ventura Publisher or The Norton Utilities. Of course, not spending money on them meant I had extra change for my antique automobile collection.

I suspect that the real reason to do right by Bill Gates has nothing to do with Bill Gates and everything to do with oneself. Though the rules are square and rationalizations come fast and furious, something sad happens when we sidestep the little decencies like paying for things.

Employees see that the bosses are cheating and feel entitled to cheat against them. Customers see that you take short cuts and wonder what short cuts you take with them. And so it goes.

We probably don't notice any striking difference in our moral life. Removing mattress tags does not lead to vehicular homicide. But that's just it—we don't notice, and we should. Then one day you are riding in the back seat of our limousine and a Harry Chapin song comes on about the moral freefall that results from these little short cuts—and you say, Hey, that's my partner Murray!

So next time a friend or family member offers to let you copy a program, do the right thing—call the SPA hotline at 800-388-7478 and turn them in. A little time in the hole will do wonders to awaken their sense of the blessed interconnectedness of things. May not do much for your relationship, though.

Better would be, next time you are offered a free ride on the latest version of the hottest and coolest and best, to just say no. Not for Bill Gates, but for you.

Lying to Ourselves

Technology is like a cancer that eats away at the souls of certain kinds of users. The manic class of users, generally including power users and questers, is prone to the worst kinds of delusions, especially in the area of technology acquisition. Believe me, I speak from experience.

telepresence—In virtual reality, this is the effect in which the user is completely immersed in the illusion created by the program. The user wears a datasuit and dataglasses, and every move he makes in real space occurs in the world he is experiencing through the computer.

test stages—Before being released to the general public, software products go through several stages. The first is the vapor stage, during which the product is merely an idea in someone's head, but the company accepts orders for it anyway. The second is the alpha stage, in which a very buggy preliminary version is sent out to important customers, to trash their data and waste their time. Then comes beta stage, in which the same process is inflicted on hundreds or even thousands of innocent people. Finally there is the official release, in which no one is spared.

user-friendly—An adjective appended to any feature in which the user has not been consulted.

When we really want something—a new modem, a program, a telephone headset, whatever—we will not rest until we have it in our hands. It doesn't matter if it means spending food money or diaper service money. Technology is like booze. We get hooked on it. We need to fill our cups. All we need, we keep saying, is one more doodad. Yet a superstoreful of doodads is never enough.

Fortunately, and understandably, most computer enthusiasts never marry. I was one of the lucky ones. I married in 1983 a highly rational, smartly assertive woman. It would be a full year before I bought my first computer, and the lies would begin.

I remember we were sitting in the living room. We had finished supper. I was reading a Radio Shack brochure that had come in the mail. I turned to Rachel and said, "Red, I have to have one of these things."

"Why?" she asked.

"Why?" That was so like her. "Honey, think of the productivity it will give my work," I explained. "Instead of endlessly doing drafts, I can finish three projects in the time one now takes." (Note: The first critical translation computer rationalizers make is from laziness to productivity. Successful computer lies lean heavily on this notion.)

The die was cast. I shelled out a hard-earned $2,700 for my first micro, a dual drive, 64K Franklin Ace

1200 with a 10 cps daisywheel printer. For weeks I reveled in its editability, its ability to print out consecutive drafts without smudges, without White-Out, without tears. I was ecstatic. For a week or so. Then I got that feeling again, a deep, shameful hankering. "Darling," I told my wife, "the more I think about it, we really need a modem."

"We do?"

I laughed. I think it was the pronoun choice. "Yes, honey. A computer without a modem is like an unfinished symphony—isolated, severed, a brain in a petrie dish. I just feel that we're not connecting; I want to reach out to the whole world of information and meet new people in strange lands. I feel this urgent social need that has heretofore gone unmet."

She looked at me funny, but she didn't say no. So I spent more money, bought a 300 bps modem. Then learned that the world of data that was out there charged by the minute like a taxicab. Once more I went to Rachel. "Sweetie, there's a brochure I'd like to show you, from the good people at CompuServe. Using this service, I'll never have to visit the library again. We can sell our encyclopedias. Just think of the parking and gas costs we'll be saving. Our car will probably last another month because of this. You know what this translates to, don't you?"

> "Computing gives us every incentive to be skeptical."
>
> *John Sculley*[6]

"Productivity, right?" Clever girl.

Well, you can imagine what has happened in the intervening decade. I have purchased four desktop PCs, plus a gift PC for my brother (who, being a dreamer, sold it), plus two laptops, four dot matrix printers, two laser printers, two scanners, five modems, two CD-ROMs and sound cards, five monitors, two fax machines, twelve telephones and three lines, a dozen mice and a switchbox in a pear tree.

I needed it all. And Rachel let me have it. In the good sense.

Here is a brief list of excellent reasons for buying hardware or software, which I commend to all manic users with a spouse to persuade:

1. **Saves steps.** New stuff tends to be more integrated than old stuff. The programs in Lotus SmartSuite interact with one another much more seamlessly and more efficiently than a hodgepodge of programs from different companies. The beauty of step-saving as a

rationale is that, if your spouse won't let you go the software route, you can try hardware. "You're right, honey, what was I thinking. I'll just get the 12 megabyte SIMMs card instead and then it won't matter what programs I'm running. What a fool I've been."

2. **Pays for itself.** Unless your yen is for a registered version of Doom II, just about any purchase can be defended as an investment.

3. **Provides a competitive advantage.** This is great if your spouse hasn't much confidence in you to begin with. "Honey, technology is my edge. If I lose that, all I have to offer is my talent." A little tough on your own self-esteem, but a trump card in a tight situation.

> "Ease and speed in doing a thing do not give the work lasting solidity or exactness of beauty."
>
> *Plutarch*[7]

4. **Takes business to a "higher level."** Weak, doddering, old computers just made you a faster typist. Sprightly, multitasking new computers may conceivably liberate you from menial tasks and free you to be the big-picture entrepreneur you always dreamed of. Great technology changes people implementers to executives! Make your own info-mercials!

5. **Prices may never be this low again.** That's a good one. Practice before a mirror so you can keep a straight face.

6. **Let's make a deal.** Tie your computer purchase (and its productivity and therefore income enhance-ments) to something your spouse wants. "Tell you what. First $100 I make with the new machine, we go shopping for that Hoover you've had your heart set on. It's a win/win deal all the way."

7. **Give me a gigabyte or give me death.** This ploy recognizes that the two most effective motivators are irrational—fear and guilt. You work hard for a living—why add to that terrible burden and possibly shorten your life expectancy, quite possibly dying alone, face mashed against a cold keyboard, by denying you a few easily affordable, productivity-enhancing tools?

Here's another technique I picked up. Package arrives by UPS. You open it up, maybe you say, "Gee, I wonder what this could be."

Inside is a new motherboard to upgrade your Pentium to a P6. Your lip starts to sweat, just thinking about the power. Spouse gives you that forlorn weary-of-the-war look. You slap your forehead. "Oh, I know what this is, it's that 30-day trial deal, whereby you get to use it for a month, then you send it back. Hey, it'll be fun operating at 120 MHz for 30 days."

Let's say spouse isn't 100 percent convinced by all this. "You're not going to keep it then?"

"Gosh, no. I'm just taking this company for a ride, honey. Oh, I suppose, if in the course of testing the thing I found that it enabled me to make staggering gains in productivity, then I might consider keeping it. But if that's so, then it pays for itself, right? Otherwise, it's no trouble at all to undo these eight screws at the back of the CPU box, disconnect every cable and wire, remove all the expansion boards, unsnap the motherboard, replace the new 860 meg hard disk I also ordered for 30 days' trial with the old one, pop the board back into the box, screw the pathetic old computer back together, and send the new one back to those poor saps. What could be easier?"

Support, particularly inexpert support, is important, especially when the subject is too technical to explain. Once Red wanted to know why it was worth $1,100 to upgrade from a 486 to a Pentium. "Let's say you're writing a column on a 486-66-2 DX," she said. "How will a faster chip speed help you finish the article any faster? How will it get you paid any faster?"

> "Expert systems represent the formalization of procedures that can be encoded into software and replicated easily and cheaply. But will these systems ever be able to codify what philosopher Michael called 'tacit knowledge'—the insights we gain from intuition and long experience?"
>
> *Daniel Bell*[8]

Now, I could have sat her down, smiled benignly, and said "Rachel, Rachel, Rachel," and told her all the complicated reasons, arithmetic included, why an increase in CPU speed enhances productivity, which creates an incremental momentum that courses throughout the entire business enterprise, with the benefits trickling directly down to our household finances. A rising tide lifts all ships, etc.

But I'd already tried that once before. Instead I just say, "Sweetheart, it has nothing to do with CPU speed. It has to do with maintaining parity with the competition. What was it Poor Richard said, 'For want of a nail, the war was lost?' You save a little here, balk at a few pennies' investment there, and one day you wake up and everyone else has gone on ahead, and left you behind, in the past, wallowing in obsolescence.

"Is that what you want, for us to go down in flames because we weren't forward-thinking enough to make a tiny investment in our future? Because if it is, I'll return this board right now, and get a refund, and we'll all of us—you, me, the kids—go shopping for metal detectors right now."

If every technique I have offered here comes to naught, if you throw your best arguments into the fray and they crash and burn, there is one last-ditch recourse, to be used only when all other attempts fail.

> "Machines have no sense of humor, and I can't stand to live in a world with no sense of humor, no sense of irony, where everything is literal. That's hell."
>
> *Paul Fussell*[9]

Tell the truth. Put all your cards on the table. Admit you have a problem with technology, that you are no longer in control of your life, that you are powerless in the face of mail order catalogs and those ultra-suave superstore sales clerks. And get down on your knees and beg for this final indulgence today, and promise upon the graves of your ancestors that you will seek out and avail yourself of professional help, and the guidance of a higher power—tomorrow.

THE SAD STATE OF COMPUTER HUMOR

I was recently asked to contribute to a book of computer humor. I must confess that I was a little put off by the request. Did the editors see me as some sort of technological court jester? Was I funny like a clown? Is that what they're saying?

The invitation suggested to me that my strategy to position myself as a serious, ultracompetent technological guru needs a little work.

But this isn't about me. It's about how a major area of our cultural life—computers and such—fits into our view of the world.

What is it about computers and technology, that we can't all join in a common belly-laugh about them?

When I think of computer humor, I instinctively think of magazine cartoons from the 1960s, in which a white-coated technician gets a funny printout from a mainframe. The joke is that the computer never seems to accept its role as servant. It wants to rule, or worse, be loved. This tradition continues today with Ziggy cartoons, which are sometimes about computers. To me, they are so formulaic, a big laugh is impossible.

Sad to say, I think I only know one funny computer joke, and it is really a people joke:

Q. What is the difference between a used car salesperson and a computer salesperson?

A. The car salesperson knows he's lying.

Why is this the only one? What topic better illustrates the profound shift we are experiencing in our society? It was obviously a topic better minds than mine have already considered.

I decided to research the topic. I TELNETed area public libraries and looked up "computer humor," "computer jokes," and "technology ribticklers" in their keyword databases. And got nothing.

I tried the Library of Congress and was luckier. There is a book called *Computer Humor*, by Donald D. Spencer, Camelot Publishing,

MILTON BERLE'S GREATEST COMPUTER JOKES [10]

A computer salesman came into a company and showed the president how his computer was more efficient than their old one. The president said, "Yours is a heck of a deal, but we can't get rid of the old one. It knows too much!"

Our company has an old computer. It runs on candles.

A young male computer and a female computer met at a computer show. The female computer offered the male an Apple. The male asked, "Is your name Eve?"

We have one man who runs programs for computers. Last week he ran *Dumbo*, and the week before, *Fantasia*.

Our computer is down so often it has canvas burns.

The company I work for is so stressful the computer has an ulcer.

They've finally come up with the perfect computer. If it makes a mistake, it blames another computer.

1994–96 pages, with 26 illustrations. Sounds like an update of my old mainframe cartoons. And this intriguing entry: *A Gep Is Ember* (*The Computer Is Human*), a compendium of winning entries in the Hungarian-based International Competition for Cartoons, published in Budapest by Neumann Jan Szamitogeptudomanyi Tarsasag, 1988.

I tried another tack, pulling a score of regular joke books from the shelves and looking up computers, technology, etc., in the indexes. I was indignant to find only about eleven jokes in over 5,000 pages. And the level of humor in these eleven was—well, read and weep:

> The company I work for is so stressful even the computer has an ulcer.
>
> Our computer is down so often it has canvas burns.

This would never do. Another possibility was the "Abort, Retry, Fail?" feature on the last page of every issue of *PC Magazine*. But this isn't really humor. It's mostly a collection of ads and headlines that show that the paste-up artist didn't know how a mouse is used or a copywriter misused some terminology. The "Abort, Retry, Fail?" section laughs at those of us struggling to keep up—the dreamers, questers, worriers, and technophobes. The Laurels and Hardys of the computer world.

When all else fails, where must one look? The Internet. I skimmed the World Wide Web for computer humor. Sure enough, there were tons of humorous home pages, funny quotations, spoofs, puns, and vignettes.

"I went out and bought an Apple computer. It had a worm in it. I tell you, I don't get no respect."

Rodney Dangerfield[11]

Problem was, it was all techie humor—you have to be an adept to get the jokes. Hundreds of Pentium jokes, hackers' daffynitions, "Bill-Gates-Goes-to-Hell" fables, hilarious error messages ("The nanobites are in full-scale rebellion!") and even more hilarious acronyms (MACINTOSH: Machine Always Crashes; If Not, The Operating System Hangs).

This stuff has its moments, but it is mostly only funny to the initiated few. If you stop and ask yourself, "Would Dickie Flatts or any average person laugh at this material?" The answer is a very sober, very emphatic no.

Which gets us to the very heart of the computer humor predicament. Technology, unlike other topics, is not a universally shared thing. If a big fat banker slips on a banana peel, everyone, except a small but robust handful in the financial community, will bust out laughing. You've got a banker, a banana, and a behind—it can't miss.

But in the world of technology, it's never certain who the bad guy is (after Bill Gates, that is), or whether the banana peel is his nemesis or ours.

Techies making fun of dumb innocent users is funny in a bitter sort of way. We've already dealt with the pain the techno naturals carry with them through life. Their scabrous humor draws on all their pain and unappreciated expertise. But it leaves the rest of us cold. Making fun of some doc-writing devil in Rangoon experimenting with the English language lets us express our frustration with bad documentation. It's cathartic. But it isn't especially funny, and an unattractive chauvinism seeps through.

ACRONYMS

Ever wonder what the letters in the computer names come from? Here are some irreverent proposals, culled from the best technological wits hanging from their toes on the entire Internet.

APPLE: As Processor Ponders, Lose Everything

DEC: Dump Everything and Close

MACINTOSH: Machine Always Crashes; If Not, The Operating System Hangs

MICROSOFT: Most Intelligent, Complete, and Rigorous Operating System OF Today

NEXT: Now EXchange for Trash

SUN: Such Utter Nonsense

WARP: What A Rotten Program

It seems to me that good humor engages pain, and the best humor reflects back on oneself. The people of the Soviet Union had a great genius for expressing their frustrations with their system in humor— they even had to stand in line to shoot Gorbachev, remember?

Wouldn't it be great if we could transmute our frustrations and resentments with our machines into that kind of earthy, robust belly-laughing humor?

Computers, because they say what we wish them to say, reveal what our wishes are. When we wrap up our little bedroom businesses in the grandeur of business-ese, we reveal our ambitions, and our insecurities. When we prattle on about the information age, and techno democracy, we reveal our deep hopes for a better, wiser, fairer world—and our determination to be the first to get there.

Or is that an impossibility in a society too split between winners and losers and too hemmed in by political correctness to thumb our noses at a blinking box?

OK, try this one. A rabbi, an elephant, and a UNIX programmer walk into a bar. . . .

WHAT INDUSTRY AND GOVERNMENT MUST DO

Study the changing nature of intellectual property in an age of data proliferation. If the old controls are slipping away, due to technology and globalization, then we need new understandings on what is and what isn't permissible. People who create things deserve to be compensated for their efforts—but the current system of royalties and protections is probably not up to the task.

> "Technology seems to be leading to an idle new world in which consumers are instantly gratified and yet never satisfied."
>
> *Anthony Ramirez*[12]

Create technological safeguards where feasible. Security experts cannot build a firewall around everything of value, but they can restrict access to people who belong in a given area and who are accountable for their behavior.

Set an example by halting "vaporware" offerings—products offered and even demonstrated before they exist, in order to evaluate consumer demand.

Companies expecting ethical behavior from their employees must first model it: by respecting the privacy of employee e-mail; by discouraging espionage, cheating, and unfair advantages; and by indicating in every way that the cultural expectations of the organization, its assignees and vendors, are of fair play and straight dealing.

WHAT YOU CAN DO IN THE MEANTIME

The computer industry, though it feasts on the proclivities of human nature, has no power to improve it. You probably can't do much about it, either. But you still have the leverage of assessment and self-correction.

- If the charge is that computing is making you less human, assess the charge as it relates to you. Do you find you are acting more like a fascist than before you began using computers? Are you crueler?

More dishonest? More prone to criminal acts? My guess is that you are not, and a lot of this is a canard laid upon us by essayists who can't find their reset buttons.

- Does your type lend itself to moral impetuousness? Obsessive types such as power users and questers have a tendency to damn the torpedoes and charge straight into ethically questionable waters. These people need to be especially careful about crossing the lines of acceptable behavior.

- If you want to use something someone else created, ask them. You will be surprised at how individuals are willing to share their knowledge—and how reluctant corporations are.

- If you don't know something, say so. In an information age, there is no shame in not having information, only for being unwilling to go get it.

- Share credit. One of the weird aspects of knowledge is that repeated truth has more credibility than original truth. If I personally mount the pulpit and declare that the end-user should have a voice in product design, people will yawn. If I say, "As quality guru Joseph Juran taught us, quality is in the eyes of the customer," people will at least give it a moment's consideration. Give credit where it is due, and it rebounds in your direction.

CHAPTER ■ 10

The Worst That Can Happen, and What If It Does

Eliminating the Distance Between Technology and User

The future is readying a raft of social and technological problems that will make today seem like the good old days; some snapshots of what is heading our way, concluding with an inspiring exhortation to get with the program

Historians love disasters, and they have been especially good at chronicling the disastrous consequences of emerging technologies. You don't need to look at recent history, Hiroshima or Chernobyl, to make this point. From the dawn of civilization, when people built bridges to cross rivers so they could communicate, trade, and learn from one another, those bridges have collapsed, leaving people to wonder what they were thinking of, trying to cross raging rivers on some crazy rope and board scaffolding.

With the rise of cities came burnable buildings and more outcries of distress with the new ways. With each advance—trains, planes, atomic energy—people have been horrified at the power unleashed. Information technology is no different.

Every technology, including those that go on to save and enhance millions of lives, goes through a period where it makes people's lives hell. After the initial shock, the suffering subsides somewhat, and people start to make peace with the ideas embedded in the new technology.

This book so far has focused on the hazards of computing in our own time—debt, disability, down time, and everyday despair. But what about the clouds still forming on the horizon, tomorrow's problems and challenges, that will make today's seem quaint?

This chapter looks at just a few of the technology waves that are still far from shore but steadily building in momentum. Some of them

180

are so outrageous and alien in concept and orientation that they strain the brain trying to "make peace" with them. How will we incorporate them into our work and lives? What will they mean to you? How will society absorb their impact? And whatever will

> # FEAR
> ## Paradox #10
> That which was supposed to comfort us instead gives us the willies.

become, in a hypertechno age, of people who are already having problems absorbing today's changes?

WHATEVER WILL BE

The near future will be like the present, only more so. Where the last fifteen years were about personal computing and personal productivity, the next fifteen or thirty will focus on networks. Imagine a world crisscrossed many, many times at every point by silvery webbing. Along this web passes every conceivable kind of information—movies, phone calls, sales pitches, love letters, video calls, on-line encyclopedias, financial information, live concerts, fax transmissions, magazine subscriptions, people buying and selling goods and services, people delivering those goods and services in digital form.

Everyone who can afford one, the top third of the social pyramid, will have a portable do-everything machine, like Dick Tracy's fabled two-way wrist radio, that will somehow know how to create, transmit, receive, and catalog all this information. Some of these folks will zip around in their fancy aircars, doing everything at once and reveling in the modernity of it all. For them, the world will be heaven.

Then there will be a middle third of the pyramid. This group will have access to these things but won't be able to use them except to do a few primitively simple things, like tell time and phone home. We'll chime in on the techno conversations

> "The future was predictable— though very few predicted it."
>
> *Allen Kay,*
> *Apple Computer research fellow*[1]

> "Remember my name, the virus says, which after all is just another way of saying, I'm alive."
>
> *Julian Dibbell*[2]

"We are becoming the servants in thought, as in action, of the machine we have created to serve us."

John Kenneth Galbraith[3]

during those occasions when we actually meet other people—but we won't really know what we're talking about. We will be techno phonies, terrified the techno naturals will see through us and expose us.

2020 Vision

Besides our hand-held gadgets, we will also have more permanent installations at home and at the office—a combination computer/entertainment center. This complex of machines will be a miniature city of inputs and outputs. Fiber-optic cable will bring the whole world in from the outside world. Keyboards, microphones, scanners, and sensors will take turns handling the data you feed in. If you are from the middle third of the pyramid, only your children will really know how to work this thing. People who are childless will have to learn how to use it by themselves or lease a child from one of a variety of certified providers.

We will be leaving electromagnetic storage media like hard and floppy disks behind. The future appears light based—lasers and fiber optics will replace the stuff we use now. Gateways through which we are now pleased to push data at 28,800 bps will open a hundred times wider and faster. Our machines will be able to access a million times the gigabyte of data today's amplest hard disks contain. Computing will occur at the speed of light. Indeed, we won't talk about "computers" at all, because everything will be computers; everything will be networked.

The office of the past was a sleepy place people spent the daylight hours at, with a water cooler and rubber tree plant, where people could hide from the world until quitting time. The office of the future may not be a place at all, but an idea. People will do much of their work at home, or at temporary remote locations—wherever they happen to be.

"When you're riding in a time machine way far into the future, don't stick your elbow out the window, or it'll turn into a fossil."

Jack Handy[4]

Despite this freedom, the work setting will be a frantic, anxious place. Very few people will have long-term jobs—mostly star performers who are just a little over the hill and look forward to working out a five-year contract without having to compete for every short-term contract that comes along.

Where our grandparents labored competently but without much information at their disposal, we will have the opposite problem, striving to appear competent in the face of all we do not know. Half the people alive will have "pages" about themselves in the global information network. This page will be your life résumé, accessible by hypertext keywords that relate to you, your work, your name, your interests.

If you are an **attorney** named **Barbara** in **Tierra del Fuego** who specializes in **personal injury** lawsuits against **mining companies**, your page can be accessed within seconds on the Net by anyone seeking an attorney with any of those bold-face keywords. Where you are doesn't matter, because lawsuits will no longer require courtrooms. Trials will be conducted by ISDN teleconference, with physical evidence corroborated at a central location and beamed out in real time to all interested parties as 3-D holographic images.

Your resume will tell readers what percentage of cases you won, what the average award was for, and what your record is for countersuits. To win a big job, you will have to be among the top twenty people in your field worldwide. And you will have to price yourself lower than the other nineteen.

SOME WELL-KNOWN VIRUSES

1530
AIDS-II
Alabama
AntiCAD
B1 (NYB)
Cascade
Cruncher
'Da Boys
Dark Avenger
DIR-2
Doom 2
Fish
Flip
Form
Friday the 13th
Frodo
Goldbug
Joker 2
Keypress 2
Jerusalem
Leprosy
Maltese
Manila
Natas
Mte (MuTation engine based viruses)
Stealth Boot_C
Stoned
Tequila
Tte (Trident MuTation engine based viruses)
Vienna
Violator
Whale
XYZ
Yankee Doodle

Those who can position themselves at the top of their category will have splendid, rewarding careers that they can retire early from. They will need to retire early because they will wear out quickly from the amount of work that comes their way.

The rest of the job market, over 90 percent of it, will fight for the scraps that remain—the less attractive, low-paying, plain vanilla contracts.

NANO, NANETTE

The eeriest trend of the future is miniaturization. As per Moore's Law, computing speed kept accelerating into the twenty-first century. Conventional silicon-based computer chips hit a wall around 1999, with the 500 MHz Intel Septum microprocessor, which ran so hot it had the unpleasant periodic side effect of bursting into flames. Then break-throughs began happening on a surprising new level—microscopic computing.

> "We do not build machines of flesh. We use our hands of flesh to build machines of wood, ceramic, steel, and plastic. We will use protein machines to build nanomachines of tougher stuff than protein."
>
> *Eric Drexler*[5]

A new science had been born. It was called nanotechnology—the science of billionths. The premise of nanotechnology was that it was possible to construct practical machines, including computers, out of protein molecules.

Nanotechnology was first proposed by Nobel physicist and celebrated genius Richard Feynman in the 1950s, but its cause was taken up in the 1980s by Stanford professor K. Eric Drexler.

The advantage of very small computers was that, being small—measured in nanometers, or billionths of a meter—they would be very fast and encounter minimal physical resistance. Since the main impeding factor in a conventional silicon microprocessor was the physical distance electrons had to travel to move through the logical gateways, Drexler saw that microscopic pathways meant faster electron travel, by a factor of 1,000 or more. Even the most primitive, earliest nanocomputers were hundreds of times faster than the Intel Septum.

Scientists at Syracuse University built the first molecular logic circuit in the 1980s. If you could see it, it looked like a wishbone, with two legs and a neck. The gate was a single, complex molecule, the size of a hemoglobin molecule, four nanometers across.

You could compare the computers of the 1990s to hydroelectric dams that stood in the path of a cascade of electrons, collecting some power but squandering most of it. The first nanocomputers, fashioned in 2007, functioned more like old-fashioned adding machines, with countless rods, levers, and wheels, all made of different kinds of protein—and still, because of their scale, tremendously efficient, outperforming the fastest supercomputers of that time.

In the year 2025, nanocomputers are at work in many industrial spheres, and computer scientists are pondering personal applications. Nanocomputers that can scour your pantry for mold or bacteria. An army of nanocomputers let loose in the office computer system, searching for viruses, knitting broken data fragments back together. Self-exponentiating microscopic computers, created in laboratories by other molecular computers are let loose to solve some of the problems the world is buckling under—problems of the environment, epidemiology, and feeding people.

SOME LESS WELL-KNOWN VIRUSES[6]

AIRLINE VIRUS: You're in Dallas, but your data is in Singapore.

ARNOLD VIRUS: Terminates and stays resident. But it'll be back.

BUREAUCRACY VIRUS: Divides your hard disk into hundreds of subunits, each of which does practically nothing, but all of which claim to be the most important part of your computer.

SIGMUND VIRUS: Your computer becomes obsessed with marrying its own motherboard.

ECONOMIST VIRUS: Nothing works, but your diagnostic software says everything is fine.

HEALTHCARE VIRUS: Tests your system for a day, finds nothing wrong, and sends you a bill for $4,500.

KEVORKIAN VIRUS: Helps your computer shut down as an act of mercy.

MENENDEZ VIRUS: Claims it feels threatened by the other files on your PC and erases them in "self defense."

TELEVANGELIST VIRUS: Claims that if you don't send it a million dollars, its programmer will take it back.

(Continued on page 186)

PAUL REVERE VIRUS: Warns you of impending hard disk attack: "Once if by LAN, twice if by C:>."

PLEDGE WEEK VIRUS: Your programs stop every few minutes to ask you for money.

PC VIRUS: Never calls itself a "virus," but instead refers to itself as an "electronic microorganism."

OLIVER NORTH VIRUS: Turns your printer into a paper shredder.

PEROT VIRUS: Activates every component in your system, just before the whole damn thing quits.

Techno naturals of the 21st century are rapturously learning to apply this exquisite technology. The rest of the world doesn't have the foggiest idea what it is or how it might be used.

THINKING MACHINES

The breakthrough office technology of the young millennium achieved what scientists could only mumble about a few years before—make a computer with truly human thinking capabilities. One whose thinking went beyond simple computation and a few logical tricks. A computer with vast amounts of data at its disposal, with great subtlety in surveying and prioritizing, the ability to do fuzzy thinking, to guess, to ponder, and surmise.

Open the pod bay door, HAL.

Instead of sitting down at your corporate desk at a conventional PC connected to an ordinary LAN, the modern business person sits at something called a Cyc terminus. A Cyc terminus is connected not to a hard disk but to an information network, the equivalent of many thousands of floppy disks' worth of information about the business they were in.

Cyc combined several dazzling computing ideas into one big box. It ran on a parallel processing engine more powerful than yesterday's supercomputers. Instead of one chip, it might have hundreds or thousands of chips. It was programmed with artificial intelligence, using a neural network model. This was an approach to idea processing that mirrored true human thought. It took computing out of its original forte, number crunching, and remade it as a subtle, fuzzy, intuitive, learning thing. This principle alone boggled the minds of the last generation.

"The easiest place to carry technology is in the mind."

Hugh Brody[7]

In a Cyc setting, the computer isn't just a filekeeper and thinking tool, it becomes a full-fledged partner, probably the most valuable partner in a business. It is a learning creature, capable of acquiring knowledge, programming itself, and creating new knowledge, new combinations, and crosscuts that humans wouldn't think of in a million megacycles.

> "I think computer viruses should count as life. It says something about human nature that the only form of life we have created so far is purely destructive. We've created life in our own image."
>
> *Stephen Hawking*[8]

At first, businesses pooh-poohed the idea. We don't have that much information, they said. But consider the sorts of nontraditional things that are all buzzing in the Cyc computer's mind at the same time:

- everything about your business: the specifications for the products you make, the processes undergirding everything, vendors you work with, the inventory, the building layout, assigned parking spaces, emergency preparations, the strategic plan, etc.;
- deep information about your business's competitors, both traditional and nontraditional, regional, domestic, and international;
- deep familiarity with past and current market conditions, so it can advise you of a course of action in a sensible, real-time way;
- information about individual employees, their skills and limitations, salaries and job classifications, evaluations, perhaps even their personalities.

Finally, the Cyc computer is imbued with a kind of structured personality. It is the kind of personality you would want in a friend— patient, wise, undemanding, always interested in you and your problems. Cyc is a Stepford computer. It can generate voice reports, ask questions, chew the fat. But it will never lie.

Unlike nanocomputers, Cyc computing is not just for techno naturals. True to the paradoxical

> "Machines are worshipped because they are beautiful and valued because they confer power; they are hated because they are hideous and loathed because they confer slavery."
>
> *Bertrand Russell*[9]

WIMP—An acronym used by the techno savvy to disparage the interface preferred by the techno averse. It stands for Windows, Icons, Mouse, and Pointer.

wish list—What users tell technology companies they would like to see in the next upgrade, and what companies include in their catalog of add-on products.

nature of computing, the most complicated technologies are among the easiest to use.[10]

THE DARK SIDE

We mentioned the top two thirds of the pyramid. There is a third, very large section comprising the base of the pyramid. This is the servant class, the techno serfs, those who can't afford technology or who are denied it or who have forsworn it. It will not be written anywhere that this group will serve the other two groups, but that will be the effective result.

In an augmented society, the unaugmented perform the chores the augmented have outgrown. They serve the sandwiches, change the lightbulbs, carry out the trash. In a society that claims to be classless, they are clearly the lowest tier.

Techno serfs will be an embarrassment to the pretensions of the information society, their lives a rebuke to the world order of better living though free information. The division between classes will be sharper than the division between white collar and blue collar.

The lower third will also include a politicized criminal class. Some of these people will have acquired outlaw technology but will not have made peace with the existing order. They will comprise an electronic militia dedicated to opposing the larger society, which they will see as weak and spoiled. The electronic militia will take virtual arms against the ultraorganized world of the Net, which they will perceive as an intolerable Big Brother.

VIRAL VIOLENCE

The talk on the top of the pyramid, at the virtual water cooler, will be about the constant threat of violence and chaos coming from the base of the pyramid. Instead of hurling bombs, people will infect one another's data assets with deadly viruses. Hollywood will make scores of movies about computer viruses. Teenagers on dates will huddle close together, wincing at the violence done to file allocation tables. Tabloid news shows will focus on the latest computer virus the way they talk today about celebrities.

This is no joke. Antivirus researchers back in 1995 were already finding 150 to 200 new viruses every month. The full list of extant, live, destructive viruses in that year topped 6,000.[12] By 2010, that many are released upon the public every month.

The bad news is, these are probably the good old days. The numbers of new viruses are ramping up every day, and despite antivirus tools and better downloading regimens, reports of infections are increasing exponentially.

Viruses can do a number of terrible things: destroy data, create bad sectors, wipe out disk space, overwrite disk directories, infect programs, and hang systems. Sometimes they are easy to detect, as when your screen locks up, and all you can see is the word GOTCHA! Subtler viruses mimic the symptoms of a dozen other problems: system slowdown, missing files, corrupted files, crashes, and reboots. Only if every machine in your office shows these same symptoms can you be confident you have a virus.

A computer virus is as alive as any amoeba or mold. It grows, replicates, travels, adapts to its surround, learns, attacks, hides, defends itself, and "eats" resources.

JABBING[11]

'Tweak brim, and the slits tow
Did gyrfalcon and gimmicks in
　the WAC:
All min were the boron,
And the moment ratification out-
　grow.

"Beware the Jabbing, my son!
The jaws that bite, the claws that
　catch!
Beware the Judaism bird, and
　shun
The frustrate Bandies!"

He took his vortex sword in hand:
Long time the many foe he sought
So rested he by the Tumult tree,
And stood awhile in thought.

And, as in UFOs thought he stood,
The Jabbing, with eyes of flame,
Came whiffs through the tulip
　wood,
And burch as it came!

One, two! One, two!
And through and through
The vortex blade went snickered-
　snack!
He left it dead, and with its head
He went galvanic back.

"And hast thou slain the Jabbing?
Come to my arms, my beams boy!
O fracas day! Callous! Called!
He chortled in his joy.

'Tweak brim, and the slits tow
Did gyrfalcon and gimmicks in
　the WAC:
All min were the boron,
And the moment ratification out-
　grow.

The latest, most dreaded virus is the computer-eating virus, which combines the electronic structure of software code with the molecular structure of sodium chloride. Once the invaders gain entry to your system, they spill off the storage device and swarm over the electronic hardware components in the system and quickly glaze every wire and contact with nonconductive table salt. The computer stops as surely and as permanently as Lot's wife.

Future viruses will be harder to detect and contain than today's mischief-makers. We already are seeing stealth viruses that mask the damage they do by creating false file masks, telling users that the corrupted files are the same size and the same date as the original files.

We will be seeing polymorphically perverse viruses. These are electronic germs that constantly mutate, changing their own code so that a system that scans and detects them once using a conventional scanning program will be unable to recognize them upon re-scan.

> "In view of all the deadly computer viruses that have been spreading lately, Weekend Update would like to remind you: when you link up to another computer, you're linking up to every computer that that computer has ever linked up to."
>
> *Dennis Miller*[13]

Viruses of the future will be both more malignant and more benign. Viruses are not hard to make and do not require enriched uranium or expensive lab equipment or even a car. There is actually commercial software available to help the nontechnical person create viruses. You do not have to leave your house to deliver one. It will be extremely simple for terrorists to launch virus strikes against networks worldwide.

Political terrorists, practical jokers, vandals, unbalanced loners, and people holding a grudge against you, for whatever reason, will have a deadly, easy-to-fire weapon held constantly to your head. It will require continuous scanning, continuous updating of your detection software, and abstemious discipline in your downloading and disk-swapping habits to hold the wee beasties at bay.

The Danger of Security

A society terrified of data attacks can be expected to clamp down on data security. The government has proposed the installation, in factories, of a "Clipper chip" in every new PC. This chip provides a standard encryption format for all the data on your hard disk. Supposedly, this encryption will protect your data from being stolen or tampered with while networking. But many PC users are up in arms over the proposal. If the entire country is using a standard encryption format, the logic goes, then busting Clipper will give thieves access to everything. Worse, in some people's eyes, is the idea of the government being the watchdog for our confidential information. Can you say police state?

> "Global incoherence is 'the sum of all fears realized.' It is a 'world adrift'—lacking leadership and the motivating vision of the future that can propel societies forward. The weight of the past proves more powerful than the inspiration of any particular future. Weapons would take on a particularly influential role in this scenario."
>
> *John L. Petersen*[14]

Let's say your company has decided its data is too precious for anyone to monkey with. What sorts of assurance do you or your company now have that no one will get into your computer, pretend they are you, and destroy or make off with your most precious data assets?

What we will see in the future will be security technologies that will take your breath away. These biometric (physical identification) technologies exist today, in high-security installations like Federal Reserve Banks and military bases. With the flood of expected viruses and data crime, they will become commonplace in ordinary offices like yours.

- **Fingerprint readers.** The task of a biometric device is to scan some unduplicatable physical part of the prospective user, such as a fingerprint, and compare what it sees against what it already knows. A typical fingerprint reader sits next to your PC connected to the serial port. It looks like a trackball, with a groove on top instead of a ball. Put your fingertip in the groove and it quickly compares the scanned image against the internal template obtained the first time you used it. Just as law enforcement officials look for ridges and patterns on fingerprints, so does this kind of system. But since its digitized template is a number, not a picture, one cannot in any way photocopy or dump it for later mischief.

■ **Retinal scanning** is the most eye-opening of the biometric technologies in use today. The user looks into a reading device that may look like a pair of binoculars. Inside the reader a dull, infrared beam bounces light against the rear wall of the eye, looking for unique blood vessel patterns. The scan waveform is then compared against a brief digital template—usually less than 100 bytes long. The whole verification process, which takes and compares multiple 480° sweeps and 192 readings, takes about two seconds. The biggest user of retinal scanners today is the Swiss Army—the people with the knives. Over 15,000 members of that country's volunteer militia are eye-printed and can be reached within moments in the event of an insurrection in the Alps.

"A computer doesn't need to seek a court warrant to monitor every aspect of your personal life. A self-training automated surveillance system doesn't need permission to observe your movements or communications."

Charles Ostman[15]

■ **Signature recognition** sounds simple, but it performs a very complex task. Our signatures, after all, are never quite the same. Scanners may analyze pen pressure, size of signature, and amount of variation from last sign-in. Some systems go the extra mile, scrambling and unscrambling your signature in storage so that it cannot be taken from the database and used.

■ **Hand geometry.** Originally developed in the late 1960s, today's hand readers scan the top, bottom, and sides of the user's hand, comparing the scan against the digitization recorded at the time of enrollment.

■ **Voice recognition.** The idea is to have the user speak a PIN or password into a phone receiver and for the voice reader to verify the scanned speech against an internal template. The computer may ask for a backup phrase in case it is uncertain of a match. The idea is attractive because it is so cheap—all you need is a phone and a reader. But bridging the gap between computers and the human voice is a tricky business. People's voices change from day to day—colds, anxiety, aging, fatigue—and voice readers must cope without allowing false positives.

There are several things people will not like about biometrics. First, it is invasive. Even in a war zone, not everyone wants their eyeballs scanned or to be fingerprinted like a felon. But false positives are a bigger problem. A good biometric scanner is sensitive enough to prevent malefactors from holding up a dead user's eyeball, or severed hand, or latex-molded finger, and gaining entry. What they trip over are false positives—disallowing people who have every right to admission. If that happens three or four or five times a day in your office, you will want to abandon your biometric security system in the nearest dark alley.

The future will throw ever more exotic security technologies at us. How about a device that scans not just your eye but your whole head? It's called a passive cranial scan—it scans you whether you want to be scanned or not. Or skincell printing—it collects shedded skin cells from your fingertip and compares that against your unique skincell waveform.

Then there's blood testing, DNA analysis, and saliva matching. Neural networks for face verification. Or the amazing biometric remembering chair that can tell, by your weight and the unique contour of your behind, whether that is really you up there.

It is all part and parcel of the world's fall from innocence. The good old days did not require remembering chairs or retinal scans. A time permeated by drugs, crime, confidence scams and terrorism, technological haves and have-nots does.

A HISTORY OF THE FUTURE

Why will the society of the future, a society that has so much to celebrate, be so angry? We can see that anger already blossoming around us today. Politicians have never been more suspect, nor the electorate angrier.

A lot of it is technology-driven. Think of desktop technology as the latest wrinkle in the evolution of democracy. Our grandparents, in the 1940s and 1950s, lived in a highly centralized society. Their role as individuals in that society was to be good units. They registered to vote, did their jobs, and let that Social Security fund grow. They were cogs in a prosperity machine, and it worked pretty well, and they didn't complain.

In the intervening decades, computers helped inflate our sense of ourselves as individuals. Decentralized technology allowed people who had never before been important to make important decisions on the job. The technology empowered and emboldened us. We began to express ourselves because we had the means to do so.

Suddenly, parties, interest groups, regional differences, economic classes, and ethnic identity weren't so important. What was important was the buzzing inside each head. We are all aflame with our own opinions and ideas, and we are aching to express them. Why wait two years for an "election" when we could elect to dial CompuServe or the Internet and tell Bill Clinton or Rush Limbaugh or Ross Perot what's on our minds this very instant?

The establishment turned up its nose at the cyber populists. They not only didn't get it, they didn't want to get it. If you wrote a crank letter to the president on the back of a grocery bag and sped by the White House and delivered it in person, you got a typed answer. If you e-mailed him a crank letter, it might be tabulated, but it wasn't responded to.

> "In the past, human life was lived in a bullock cart; in the future it will be lived in an aeroplane. And the change of speed amounts to a difference in quality."
>
> *Alfred North Whitehead*[16]

When we learned that we could stand up to politicians, politicians lost power. Society began to fragment into bitterly divided interest groups. Despite, or perhaps because of, all the information at our fingertips, each group chose to focus on information that best explained its predicament. Paranoia and misinformation drove the camps even farther apart.

The cyberspace lit up with quarreling and personal attacks. We could log onto some bulletin board and bash antlers with some nabob of the opposite persuasion as us. Soon a crowd would gather, egging us on. You didn't have to be smart to be heard on the Net—you just had to be able to type.

Eventually, groups like the electronic militia broke away from society entirely, went underground, and began mounting targeted strikes using viruses and data bombs.

DEAR LANDLORD

Looking back, was there anything people living in, say, the 1990s could have done to keep this bad science fiction movie from becoming reality?

The problem of the future I described is not technology but access to technology. Either it is too expensive, or some people are forcibly excluded, or they are too fearful, for whatever reason, to join the Net. The way to keep society from splitting down the middle into techno haves and have-nots is to make sure the have-nots have a fair chance to learn technology and be part of the game.

That is the impetus behind House Speaker Newt Gingrich and President Clinton's trial balloons about putting laptop computers in the hands of people in poverty. Surely the upside of such an idea is that a giant part of our population won't get permanently left behind in the changing economy. People can use PCs to help in their education, to learn skills, to help find jobs, to create businesses, to perform work itself, and to network in their chosen fields.

But there are downsides, too. A laptop give-away program, such as Clinton described, would cost tens of billions of dollars the first year, and billions more in subsequent years, as machines are replaced or upgraded. Gingrich's plan, by contrast, only called for tax credits for poor people. This would be cheap for the government but unlikely to be very effective, since people in poverty who don't pay taxes are not likely to shell out thousands of dollars for the sake of reducing their taxes.

> "We don't know where this is heading. We didn't know 25 years ago. And we don't know now. We're feeling our way in a new world."
>
> *Leonard Kleinrock,*
> *co-inventor of The Internet*[17]

Worse than the money is the political cost such a program would carry. Not all Americans will cotton to the idea of giving poor people something very valuable, for free, that cost them many weeks of hard work to purchase on their own.

So we have a gruesome choice to make: insist that the poor buy their own computers, which they are not likely to do in meaningful numbers, or swallow hard and write the check that drafts them into the information age and decreases the chance of the cyberpunk future described here.

The best solution might be to help people without much money buy equipment that costs less—used machines, liquidated, and obsolete models. You can find an old AT system with monitor and dot-matrix printer in the classifieds for as little as $300. No, it won't run Windows 95 or Netscape, so it will be a tough training vehicle. But it's something.

The other thing we can all do is learn to treat one another with greater respect. There is so much antagonism in the air these days, and so many politicians and other interests who seem to acquire power by pitting one group against another. Why not make a promise to ourselves to ignore the whole idea of groups altogether and approach one another as individuals we don't know, with no strikes against them.

We can commit random acts of techno kindness. Encouraging one another to become independent and able to prosper. Tutoring people who know less than we do about a technology or program. Sharing equipment we no longer need.

The great thing about trends is that they swing back and forth. That means we can fight the trend toward rudeness, aggressive behavior, and techno violence. When BBSing, count to ten, or even higher, if you feel your temperature rising in a debate. Remember that flamebaiting—our grandparents called it "getting somebody's goat"—is just a plea for attention. Just because you cannot see the person you are speaking to is no excuse for dehumanizing them.

> "On a clear disk you can seek forever."
>
> *Anonymous*

Give the other fellow and his ideology the benefit of the doubt. Perhaps the great poet Bob Dylan, never appreciated in his own time as an avatar of computer wisdom, said it best, in his song "Dear Landlord":

"If you don't underestimate me, I won't underestimate you."

The Ultimate Technology

We began this book talking about the painful distance most users feel from time to time between themselves and their machines. We conclude with a vision of this distance being finally resolved. At first it will sound like the technophobe's worst nightmare. In fact, it may turn out to be the technophobe's best chance for salvation. Or maybe it is the nightmare after all—I can't quite make this one out.

Where nanocomputing was about creating computers out of molecules, biocomputing goes even smaller—much smaller in fact, to the individual electron. This should not be completely surprising. Computers are basically just arrays of switches for streams of electrical current.

The early computer scientists used mechanical relay switches— little clicking clothespins. But the technology was bent on miniaturization from the very beginning. Soon the mechanical switches gave way to electrical switches, which gave way to vacuum tubes, and then transistors, and then micro-etched silicon switchbeds—today's microprocessors.

What could be a more logical development than a switch that goes on and off with the admittance of a single electron? An atomic or quantum computer would have zero impedance and be superconductive. It would be fast as the dickens to the 20th power.

They are doing it. In 1990 scientists at IBM proved they can move individual atoms around in 1990, when they precisely aligned 35 xenon atoms to form an IBM logo.

This is a way tinier level than nanocomputer scientists talk about. Once we get these quantum computers going, we'll have taken computing as far from the desktop as it could possibly go.

An even more intriguing possibility is mind-controlled computers. A 1995 article in *The New York Times* detailed an experiment in which human beings were able to move cursors across a screen using their brain waves. They were operating regular desktop PCs like you and I

1976. Wouldn't this have made a classic Volkswagen ad? The Apple I, the first of a total of sixty built in Stephen Wozniak's dad's garage, with the proceeds from the sale of Wozniak's old VW beetle. Hippie Steve Jobs and nerd Steve Wozniak change the world with their little box.

1979. WordStar and VisiCalc, the first two killer PC applications. Both are tragic success stories. MicroPro's WordStar was developed by genius programmer John Barnaby. When Barnaby left the company in 1985, the product ruled the world— but the company could not figure out how to adapt the code Barnaby left behind in the confusion. WordPerfect leaped ahead of it to become the standard DOS word processing program. In VisiCalc, designed for the Apple II, Dan Bricklin invented the electronic spreadsheet and revolutionized the way people think about and work with financial numbers. As with WordStar, VisiCalc was unable to make the crossing to the world of the IBM PC, and the glory and profits of true business computing went to Mitch Kapor and his DOS-based Lotus 1-2-3.

(Continued on page 198)

1981. Adam Osborne, a charismatic visionary, unleashed his Osborne 1, the world's first portable computer, upon the world. The affordable CP/M-based Osborne takes the world by storm, but the company goes bankrupt anyway—the bragging rights for portable computing going to Compaq's DOS-based machines.

1982. IBM unveils its PC in 1982 but fails to lock up rights to the computer's two most prized technologies—its operating system, MS-DOS, and it microprocessor, the Intel 8088 chip. This failure is the single biggest business goof in history.

1984. Apple Computer announces its Macintosh computer, in a legendary Orwellian Superbowl commercial in January. In the underpowered, overdue, overpriced Macintosh, the vision of computerized augmentation Douglas Engelbart described in the 1960s is finally revealed.

use, just by using their minds.[18] It's cybertelekinesis, and you read it in the *Times*, not some Stephen King novel.

The thrust of this particular research is extremely down-to-earth. It is an effort to empower paralyzed people to use computers. But imagine what the future holds for us if we can fully internalize the idea of computer control. You think a thing, and the thing happens.

Through the Looking Glass

This chapter is ending this book much the same way that falling down into the tree began *Alice's Adventures in Wonderland*, but the sensations produced should be about the same. Disorientation, overload, craziness—the very things I promised to make go away 200 pages ago.

The change is unnerving. The crashes, errors, and erasures are as gut-wrenching as they ever were. Your career is unstable; it is like trying to work in a blender. Life is unfair and later you die. And The Andy and Bill Show is always on—hardware creating new product opportunities for software and vice versa, all with an eye toward relieving you of your hard-earned filthy lucre.

But be honest—isn't it interesting? Isn't it neat? Isn't it fun? Whether you are a techno natural or a true technophobe, whether your computer is your friend or your nemesis, you must admit you live in the most remarkable of times. And you must sometimes get a shiver from the effortlessness of doing something that grandma and grandpa never dreamed of doing or could do only with sweat on the brow and a kink in the back.

When I began writing this book something happened that, now that I think back, foretold this page. It was Christmas evening, and the regular football season was coming to an end. My team, the Vikings, was tied for first place with three other teams in their division. Depending on the outcome of the game in progress between the Lions and Dolphins, my team would finish anywhere from first to fourth place. The Lions had narrowed the score to 27-20, with a few minutes left to play. But I was bushed after a long day of ripping and tearing and trudged off to bed.

All night I dreamed I was trying to learn the final score. At first I tried to tune in a TV. No news program was on. I turned on the radio and got ferocious static. Damn sunspots. I dialed the local sports information 976 number. The line was dead. Things were getting eerie. I booted up my PC in this dream and tried CompuServe's AP Online service. The score had still not been updated! I called my Internet gateway, which also had a news service. But wouldn't you know it, I couldn't make a connection with the network.

> "Can you tell me, please, which way I ought to go from here, asked Alice. That depends a good deal on where you want to get to, said the cat."
>
> *Lewis Carroll*[19]

At this point I was in a frenzy of wanting to know the score and frustrated that nothing was working. But then I got this idea: why not use my body as a computer, like in that *New York Times* article, and get the information simply by asking my body to link up with all the other information points in the world—everyone else.

Sure, it had never been tried before, but why wouldn't it work? So I kind of crossed my eyes and focused on networking, and darned if I didn't start getting incoming messages from other sources. I could access people's memories, their emotions, even the books in their libraries and the data on their computers.

It worked. It was natural. I didn't need to install anything, I didn't need to study any schematics, I didn't need to read any documentation or view any demos. I didn't have to flip any toggles, jumpers, or DIP switches. If I wanted something, I got it. That was all there was to it.

I used to dream I could fly. Now I was dreaming I could network and compute, without an actual computer. I became very excited by my dream discovery. It meant we finally had a way of communicating and moving information that didn't make us all crazy. A human network, with no one in charge, no dues to pay, no help files, no buttons to push. I should come up with some great name for my discovery and trademark it.

But it was just a dream. When I woke up, I tried focusing my powers. Nothing happened. The power had gone out of me. Humankind did not have a "Force" it could glom onto to know all it needed to know. Or at least I couldn't find it.

Still, the idea haunts me. What if technology were to stop hurting people, stop dividing us against one another, stop peeling money from our pockets like ripe bananas, and just generally stopped making us feel stupid and backward and afraid?

"Things should be as simple as possible, but not simpler."

Albert Einstein[20]

I think we all have to keep the faith. PCs were invented by hippies, after all, not demons. Day by day and year by year, the people who make these things roll the ball of usable technology closer to us. Someday, maybe, they'll roll it all the way to our doorstep and implant it in our brain. Once it's in your brain, even the technophobe becomes a techno natural, because that's what it is. Techno, natural.

Till then, we have to meet it halfway.

NOTES

INTRODUCTION

1. This beloved remark of Robert X. Cringley appeared in a 1988 editorial in *InfoWorld*. It appeared again in his book *Accidental Empires*, Addison-Wesley, 1992.
2. I should also post a more temperate letter from a technology worker who agreed with the letter I printed but expressed it more gently:

    "I work in internal tech support. I should say up front that if I didn't like helping users I wouldn't be in this job. But it can get extremely annoying to have ten people interrupting you to ask how to save a document in MS Word when you've got a total collapse of your network in progress and every machine in the lab is about to crash when the file server goes down without warning. Working in tech support is a no-win situation, and that is bound to frustrate a lot of people. The hostility you've seen is only a better-concealed version of the hostility so often found among people in customer-service types of jobs. But because tech support people in business would get fired if they openly displayed such hatred for users, the feelings of malevolence come out only in private or explicitly noncommercial forums, like e-mail and alt.folklore.computers."
3. Quote courtesy of T. A. Melander, from his recollection on Usenet of a discussion by Mr. Campbell at Sarah Lawrence University.
4. Henry David Thoreau, *Walden*, found on The Gutenburg Project, The Internet.
5. Appeared in a Morris County, N.J., newspaper, September 17, 1987.
6. Downloaded from a wonderful World Wide Web resource, Rand Lindsly's Huge Quotation File, http://pubweb.ucdavis.edu/documents/quotations/rand.html
7. Mary McGrory, "The Laptop and I," *Washington Post*, May 24, 1992, p. C2.
8. Allen Ginsberg, the first lines of his great poem *Howl*. City Light, 1952.
9. Eric was for many years a contributing editor of *Computer User*. He is author or co-author of numerous books about Xwindows and other technical topics. This quote was given to me by Eric's sometime collaborator, Kevin Reichard.
10. Lindsly.
11. Steven Levy, *Insanely Great*, Penguin Books, 1995.

CHAPTER 1

1. *InfoCulture*, Steven Lubar, Houghton Mifflin, 1993, p. 122.
2. Levy.
3. Lindsly.

4. Colin Jarman, *The Guinness Book of Poisonous Quotes*, Contemporary Quotes, 1993.
5. Lindsly.
6. I invited readers of the alt.quotations Usenet newsgroup to help me with quotations about computer technology. Basically, I got the same half dozen familiar quotations, repeated many times over. I received seven variations on this remark of Pablo Picasso, reportedly from a *Life* Magazine interview.
7. List inspired by "Hollywood and Computers," on the World Wide Web at http://fs1.itdean.umn.edu/cbi/movies.htm

Chapter 2

1. William Edwards Deming, *The New Economics*, MIT Center for Advanced Engineering Study, 1993, p. 2.
2. Lindsly.
3. John Bear, *Computer Wimp*, Ten Speed Press, 1983.
4. Lindsly.
5. Watney's Red Barrel is the *nom de BBS* of a colleague of mine on Ivory Tower Bulletin Board, Minneapolis.
6. Don't worry if you don't neatly fit any of them. You may see yourself as an amalgam of two or more types, or a type not described, or a type unique to yourself. Or you may see yourself as the type of person who snorts derisively at the idea that people can be categorized by type. That's OK. It's a type, but it's—OK.

    In fact, to prove my flexibility on this point, let's add a quick half-dozen more types:

    The *specialist*—a user who is adept at one aspect of technology but useless at every other aspect. I know advanced software developers who are great at their own niche but fumble-fingered when a question relates to the hardware their software runs on.

    The *dabbler*—a user who likes technology, isn't afraid to try new things, but isn't able to (or doesn't need to) stick with anything long enough to acquire real mastery of it. The dabbler is like someone described as Dwight Eisenhower's knowledge base—miles across and an inch deep.

    The *dyslexic*—she is not clinically dyslexic, but she really cannot seem to deal with the learning materials at hand. The books don't "speak her language" or aren't organized to suit her. So she doesn't use them.

    The *miser*—always on the lookout for a bargain, this user puts no premium on any aspect of technology except cost. Time and again he has bought a major system on price points—and been unhappy with other aspects after he got it home and tried to make it work.

    The *hothead*—a user who could be much more adept at programming VCRs, etc., if only he were more patient. When things go wrong with a product, as they often do because of his impatience, he goes on a spuming tirade against the user-unfriendliness of that product, the company that makes it, and the genetic make-up of its executive officers.

The *sloth*—he simply can't be bothered to crack the manual. Instead he gets on the phone to his guru and has the guru painstakingly walk him through every situation. This fellow is remarkable. Two years after buying a new system, the guru is shocked to be asked how to copy a file from one disk to another. (Burned out customer support professionals think there are millions of sloths, that they are the predominant user subspecies, but it is probably just the same two hundred people, calling over and over again. I hope.)

7. I saw this quote, and the one following it, by Linda Gloya, in a presentation by Richard Tanner Pascale at The Masters Forum in Minneapolis, March 1995.

8. *CPA Software News*, February/March 1995.

9. Associated Press wire file, February 16, 1995.

10. Pascale.

11. Indeed, the country is run by near-technophobes. Only a dozen members of Congress have e-mail boxes at this time, and it is doubtful that more than two or three of those know how to use it.

12. Robert Heinlein, from "The Notebooks of Lazarus Long," *Time Enough for Love*.

CHAPTER 3

1. This is a verbatim sentence from the documentation for an expansion card I bought.

2. Lindsly.

3. Lindsly.

4. Quoted in a column by Ron Alexander, "New Yorkers, Etc.," *The New York Times*, January 6, 1991, p. E26.

5. Rowan and Martin's Laugh-In.

6. $200 million figure comes from a get-rich-quick book by despised net pioneers and immigration lawyers Canter and Siegel, who infuriated millions when they uploaded their "green card legal services" onto every single one of Usenet's over 5,000 newsgroups. Predictably, they hawk their book right on the net.

7. "Internet Smaller Than Supposed," Associated Press, May 2, 1995; interview with Matrix News editor John Quarterman.

CHAPTER 4

1. Lindsly.

2. Ian Reinecke, *Electronic Illusions*, Penguin, 1984.

3. I noticed this as part of someone's signature on Usenet. Whoever you were, thanks.

Chapter 5

1. Egil Juliussen and Karen Petska-Juliussen, *Computer Industry Almanac* 1994-95, p. 397.
2. Christopher Cerf and Victor Navasky, *The Experts Speak*, Pantheon Books, 1984, p. 208-9.
3. William Bridges, "The End of the Job," *Fortune*, September 19, 1994, p. 62.
4. Stan Augarten, *Bit by Bit*, Ticknor & Fields, 1984, p. 3.
5. Lindsly.
6. Alvin Toffler, *Future Shock*, Bantam Books, 1970, p. 145.
7. Lindsly.
8. Lindsly.

Chapter 6

1. Terry R. Dettmann and Susan Futterman, *Using CompuServe to Make You Rich*, Waite Group Press, 1995.
2. Juliussen and Petska-Juliussen, p. 297.
3. Juliussen and Petska-Juliussen, p. 297.
4. Dettmann and Fuherman.
5. Lindsly.
6. Peter G. Neuman, *Computer Related Risks*, Addison-Wesley Publishing Company, 1995, p. 165.
7. Joel Kurtzman, "International Digital Exchange," *International Journal of Commerce*, Vol 23, No. 6, Summer 1992, p. 112.
8. Robert Byrne, *The Second 637 Best Things Ever Said*, Fawcett Crest, 1986, p. 117.
9. Dettman and Futterman.
10. Supposedly from *Late Night with David Letterman*, but it doesn't seem quite Lettermanlike, does it? I found this in several home pages on the World Wide Web.

Chapter 7

1. Winn L. Rosch, "Does Your PC—Or How You Use It—Cause Health Problems?" *PC Magazine*, November 26, 1991, p. 491.
2. Godnig and Hacunda.
3. Reprinted from *CPU: Working in the Computer Industry*, Issue 12, Nov. 30, 1994.
4. From newspaper reports, January 13, 1964.

5. For an excellent short book on this topic, I recommend *Computers and Visual Stress,* by Edward C. Godnig, O.D., and John S. Hacunda, Abacus Books, 1991.
6. Lindsly.
7. Lindsly.

CHAPTER 8

1. Journal entry, January 3, 1861.
2. *Midsummer Night's Dream,* act ii. sc.1.
3. Of course, the very same day, March 1, 1995, I read that glaciers on the South Island of New Zealand have recently sped up and were galloping along at a rate of 10 meters a day—clear evidence that a new ice age has begun. So, what do I know.
4. Dennis Hayes, "Ozone Wars," *Mother Jones,* April-May 1990, p. 55; also "Behind the Silicon Curtain," *Whole Earth Review,* Summer 1990, p. 59.
5. Lindsly.

CHAPTER 9

1. Craig Broad, *Techno Stress,* Addison-Wesley Publishing Company, 1984.
2. Sean Guitton, *The Pope Speaks,* Meredith Press, 1968.
3. Lindsly.
4. Richard Saul Wurman, *Information Anxiety,* Bantam Books, 1990. p. 293.
5. Geoffrey Chaucer, "The Marchantes Tale," Line 585. *The Canterbury Tales.* From Bartlett's Familiar Quotations Online, World Wide Web.
6. Owen W. Linzmayer, *The Mac Bathroom Reader,* Sybex, 1994.
7. *Plutarch: Life of Pericles,* downloaded from the Internet's Project Gutenberg.
8. Lindsly.
9. Jon Vinocur, ed, *The Portable Curmudgeon,* New American Library, 1987. p.163.
10. Milton Berle, *Milton Berle's Private Joke File,* Crown, 1989.
11. Rodney Dangerfield, quoted from the author's memory, from an appearance on *The Tonight Show,* circa 1984.
12. Anthony Ramirez, "Techno-Indulgence as Sin," *The New York Times,* January 12, 1994, p. C7.

CHAPTER 10

1. Linzmayer.
2. Julian Dibbell, "Viruses Are Good for You," *Wired,* February 1995, p. 13.
3. Lindsly.

4. *Deep Thoughts*, by Jack Handy, appeared originally on Saturday Night Live; located as a textfile on the World Wide Web.

5. Eric Drexler, *Engines of Creation*, Doubleday, 1986; and *Unbounding the Future*, Morrow, 1991.

6. Tom Regan, Halifax, Nova Scotia, *The Daily News*, posted on the Internet.

7. Lindsly.

8. Lindsly.

9. Bertrand Russell, *Sceptical Essays*. Found in Margaret Miner and Hugh Rawson's *The New International Dictionary of Quotations*, Signet, 1993, p. 420.

10. John L. Peterson, *The Road to 2010*, Waite Group Press, p. 43.

11. This is a put-on of Lewis Carroll's already nonsensical poem, "Jabberwocky," generated by running the original through a word processor's spellchecker and using the alternates the program suggested for some of Carroll's unusual words. Posted on Usenet by Doug Landauer. Doug Landauer also was helpful in helping me define "newbie."

12. Dr. Solomon's News Release, April 24, 1995. Technopolis Communications, Burlington, MA. technopolis@aol.com.

13. Dennis Miller, "*Saturday Night Live* Weekend Update."

14. Peterson.

15. Charles Ostman, "Total Surveillance: Your Life on a Chip," *Mondo 2000*, Issue 13, p. 16; quoted in *Cybernetics Digest*, January 1995 issue, December 22, 1994.

16. Alfred North Whitehead, *Science and the Modern World*. Macmillan, 1925, p. 421.

17. Bob Pool, "Inventing the Future: UCLA Scientist Who Helped Create Internet Isn't Done Yet," *Los Angeles Times*, August 11, 1994, p. B1.

18. "Computers may soon be able to read a person's thoughts." *The New York Times*, March 8, 1995.

19. Lewis Carroll, *Through the Looking Glass*, from the Internet Gutenberg Project.

20. Lindsly.

INDEX

Benedict Arnold

THE TRAITOR WITHIN

building political alliances with government figures who could provide support. His friendship with his father-in-law could have been a useful first step since Samuel Mansfield was high sheriff of New Haven County and could have provided introductions, but Arnold was not interested. This go-it-alone attitude turned out to be a serious mistake. His military career was to suffer frequently because he had no well known men in government to speak for him.

He did display a sort of political awareness in developing opposition to British Customs policy—an opposition joined by practically all colonial merchants. For these men, smuggling became a necessity in order for them to make a living. They did not consider smuggling to be a crime, but rather an act of patriotism; since they had no voice or vote in the creation of those taxes, the customs duties were not legal, so smuggling was not illegal.

The first sign of deep political conviction was in his response to the Boston Massacre in 1770. He was horrified by the shooting of five unarmed Bostonians by British soldiers, then further outraged when the soldiers were found not guilty. "Good God!" he wrote, "are the Americans all asleep and tamely giving up their liberties, or are they all turned philosophers that they don't take immediate vengeance on such miscreants."5.

Over the next five years, the dispute between Great Britain and her thirteen American colonies grew steadily worse. In December 1773, a band of Patriots took part in a widespread protest against British East India Company tea by dumping a shipment of it into Boston Harbor. The British responded swiftly. The port of Boston was ordered closed until the tea should be paid for. Thomas Gage arrived with 3,500 redcoats to enforce this and several other new laws, known as the Coercive Acts (or, in America, the Intolerable Acts).

Arnold became determined to be a major figure in any military action that developed. Perhaps gaining military prominence was a way to restore the honor of the family name. The first step was to form a militia unit in New Haven. His offer was approved and his men were delighted with their dashing new uniforms, designed by their commanding officer—Captain Arnold.

The early years of Benedict Arnold's story displayed a pattern that would be repeated throughout his life. Until his mid-teens, he seemed to be on a path